A Social Worker's Guide to Evaluating Practice Outcomes

A Social Worker's Guide to Evaluating Practice Outcomes

Bruce A. Thyer and Laura L. Myers

Council on Social Work Education
Alexandria, Virginia

Library of Congress Cataloguing-in-Publication Data

Thyer, Bruce A.
     A social worker's guide to evaluating practice outcomes / Bruce A. Thyer and Laura L. Myers.
     p. cm.
     Includes bibliographical references.

ISBN: 978-0-87293-126-8 (alk. paper)

1. Social service--Evaluation. I. Myers, Laura L. II. Title.
     HV41.T56 2007
     361.3'2068--dc22

Printed in the United States of America on acid-free paper that meets the American National Standards Institute Z39-48 Standard.

Council on Social Work Education, Inc.
1725 Duke Street, Suite 500
Alexandria, VA 22314-3457
www.cswe.org

We respectfully dedicate our efforts in preparing this book to Alisa Rosenbaum, one of the most inspiring teachers we have ever encountered.

> any attempt to roughly gauge our effectiveness in social work and to direct changes in our practices, and perhaps even in our goals, does not mean that a rigid science will supercede a warm and soul-satisfying art. We need not fear that we will be less effective in the knowledge of our weaknesses and in the conservation of our strengths. The art and science of social work must blend if we are to serve humanity with love and with ever-increasing understanding.

> Eleanor T. Glueck
> (1936, p. 27)

Contents

Preface

We prepared this book as a helpful resource for social work students, both graduate and undergraduate, and for social work practitioners who seek a relatively simple introduction to the topic of empirically evaluating the outcomes of their own practice or of the programs provided by their agencies. A concern with determining the outcomes of social work services has long preoccupied our discipline, and rightly so. It certainly antedates the startling and disturbing comprehensive reviews prepared by Steven Segal (1972) and Joel Fischer (1973, 1976) that disclosed to public scrutiny the flimsiness of the evidentiary foundations of social work. Although reactions to these reviews were decidedly mixed, one laudable one was to encourage social workers to roll up their sleeves and more vigorously set about designing and completing credible evaluation studies of our services. These efforts paid off. Now, in the early years of the 21st century, more randomized controlled studies on the effectiveness of social work appear in print in a single year than appeared during all the years prior to 1970.

There are a number of other books dealing with the topic of evaluating practice. We are especially fond of *Program Evaluation: An Introduction* by Royse, Thyer, Padgett, and Logan (2006). The distinguished team of Bloom, Fischer, and Orme (2006) has authored *Evaluating Practice: Guidelines for the Accountable Professional*, and this is a wonderfully comprehensive volume, but its 700 plus pages focused exclusively on measurement issues and the use of single-case research designs may prove a bit intimidating for some to digest (although we enjoyed every morsel). At a little over 150 pages, Tony Tripodi's (1994) *A Primer on Single-Subject Design for*

Clinical Social Workers, like Bloom et al., focuses on single-case designs and ignores the use of group-research methods to evaluate practice. Yet there are many occasions when social workers can undertake simple outcome studies using group-research designs, and the present volume presents both methods in a fairly even-handed approach, we hope. We have tried to strike a balance between the virtues of simplicity and practicality, on the one hand, and the sins of oversimplification and lack of rigor, on the other. We thus present a variety of real-life examples of evaluating social work practice, ranging from those fairly low on the scale of internal validity to those that are pretty rigorous, recognizing that inadequate resources may prevent practitioners from frequently undertaking the strongest forms of evaluation. We have also stressed that this is OK. It is always better to have data from a simple outcome study than to have no data at all, so long as one's conclusions are appropriately circumspect. Obviously the names and identities of all clients described in this book have been suitably disguised. We hope that you will enjoy this modest volume, and we encourage readers to provide us (via e-mail to bthyer@mailer.fsu.edu) with your comments and suggestions to improve our future writing.

Bruce A. Thyer
Laura L. Myers
Tallahassee, Florida

A Brief Overview of Evaluation Research

SOME BACKGROUND ON EVALUATING PRACTICE OUTCOMES

There are many facets to evaluation research apart from the assessment of client outcomes. For example, consumer satisfaction studies examine the degree to which our clients judge that they have been helped (which is not always congruent with other indicators of change, such as more objective indicators of problem resolution). The conduct of client or community needs assessments is another form of evaluation research, as are process studies examining the presumptive mechanisms of change by which social work interventions exert their beneficent effects. Yet another type of evaluation of social work consists of some sort of administrative review of case records, an audit, if you will, of the degree to which required documents or other information is contained in records. However, in this small book, we will be exclusively focused on presenting various methods of evaluating the *outcomes* of social work intervention. While we recognize that this is not the only type of evaluative research needed by our profession, we believe that such studies are among the most important that we, as a field, can undertake. More on this latter point in succeeding pages.

The evaluation of social work treatment can be initially conceived as trying to obtain credible answers to one or more questions, questions ranging in difficulty from the apparently simple to the exceedingly complex. Here is one such set of questions that are often of keen interest to the social work practitioner:

1. Did the clients get better?

2. Did the clients improve more, relative to what would have been expected with no treatment?

3. Did the clients improve more, relative to what would have been expected with a credible placebo treatment or nonprofessional care?

4. Did the clients improve more, relative to what would have been expected if they had received treatment as usual?

5. Were any improvements long lasting?

6. Were there meaningful improvements in other areas of the clients' lives (e.g., quality of life) besides those that were the specific focus of treatment?

7. Were there any negative side effects or consequences to treatment?

8. How does the intervention work?

We will suggest in this volume that a program of evaluation research is best undertaken along similar lines. First, try to demonstrate that clients who receive a given intervention do indeed improve. Then, and only then, should you try to address the subsequent questions in the above list, an endeavor that could roughly follow the order in which we have laid them out. After answering question number one, then address number two, and see if the improvements were better than those that are found without having the treatment. Many psychosocial problems wax and wane simply with the passage of time or with the ebb and flow of environmental stressors. It is important to demonstrate that social work clients improve more through receipt of our professional services than if they had simply allowed for the passage of time. Then there are the potentially positive effects of what have variously been called nonspecific treatment effects or the placebo factor, the soothing influence of knowing that you are in good hands and receiving some sort of plausible assistance. We would hope that a professional social worker's clients would be better off than clients receiving care at the hands of a nonprofessionally trained helper. Such hopes are not always fulfilled.

For example, at one mental health center, 160 troubled children were randomly assigned to receive psychotherapy from professionally trained psychotherapists such as psychologists, social workers, or nurses or to receive academic tutoring by graduate students or elementary school teachers. Treatment lasted about two years and involved an average of 60 sessions of psychotherapy or 53 sessions of tutoring. A number of reliable and valid measures of psychosocial functioning were administered to the children before the study began and at the end of the study. Fortunately, it was found that the children receiving legitimate psychotherapy experienced significant improvements in their psychosocial functioning. This, of course, was a desirable outcome. Curiously, though, the children who received academic tutoring experienced similar improvements in psychosocial functioning, demonstrating the apparent equivalence of low-cost, nonprofessional tutoring to high-cost professional psychotherapy (see Weiss, Catron, Harris, & Phung, 1999).

The above study demonstrates that the apparent equivalence of professional and nonprofessional or placebolike intervention (we would not have predicted that simple academic tutoring would produce improvements in mental health, at least not to the extent obtained by trained psychotherapists) is not an isolated finding. Strupp and Hadley (1979) randomly assigned 30 college undergraduates troubled with anxiety or depression to two sets of "therapists." One set of therapists was highly experienced and professionally trained doctoral-level psychotherapists (average length of practice experience was 23 years) and the other therapists were equivalently educated college professors (e.g., doctoral level) with no professional training or experience in the conduct of psychotherapy. The students who received psychotherapy from trained professionals demonstrated significant improvements. This is good. However, the students who received "psychotherapy" from the nonprofessionally trained college professors improved just as much. One would hope that social services provided by professionally trained social workers would somehow be more effective than similar services provided by individuals lacking such professional training, and, to some extent, our entire system of professional training is justified by this assumption. But assumption it is and will likely remain as such until suitably controlled studies can be designed and undertaken to test these assumptions. Such demonstrations are important since at least one initial quasi experiment has looked at the effectiveness of child welfare services provided by social workers versus individuals with non-social work degrees hired into similar child welfare positions and found that individuals with bachelor of social work (BSW) and master's of social work (MSW) degrees were not evaluated by their supervisors as superior workers (Perry, 2006).

We can be pretty sure that in each of the above examples, the professionally trained social workers and psychotherapists were themselves confident that the services they were providing were not only helping their clients, but were in some significant manner of greater assistance than services provided by supposedly less-capably trained individuals. Yet, the actual results evaluating these services did not reveal this to be the case. Our field is replete with examples wherein the services provided by social workers turned out to be very effective indeed, but the converse is also true. Many studies have shown that sometime what we do turns out to be ineffective and, indeed, sometimes harmful (Fischer, 1976). In one classic study on the effectiveness of casework services provided by MSWs over a one-year period to senior citizens, it was found that clients receiving professional social work care had a higher mortality rate than the clients who got services from non-social workers (Blenkner, Bloom, & Nielsen, 1971). This was a most unexpected and indeed shocking finding, and the lesson for all of us is that we cannot blithely assume the benignant effects of social work care.

Professional social work has a long tradition of conducting systematic evaluations of the outcomes of our services, with one of the earlier such studies being a long-term outcome study of children who had been placed in foster homes (van Senden Theis, 1924). This important work involved the follow-up of over 900 children and has rarely, if ever, been replicated. Additional pioneering evaluation work was carried out by Heckman and Stone (1947), Powers and Witmer (1951), and Meyer and Borgatta (1959), with some of these early outcome studies being reviewed in 1962 by Anne Shyne. While we may debate whether our field has devoted sufficient attention to the evaluation of social work practice (most writers suggest that we have not), there is no doubt that from, the very beginnings of our profession, such efforts have been seen as of crucial importance. Bloom et al. (2006) cite one such statement from Dr. Richard Cabot in 1931 in his address at a national social work convention:

> I appeal to you. . . measure, evaluate, estimate, appraise your re-
> sults, in some form, in any terms that rest on something beyond

faith, assertion, and "illustrative case." State your objectives and how far you have reached them... Let enough time elapse so that there may be some reasonable hope of permanence in the results which you state. The greatest value [of evaluation of practice] will be... an evaluation of one method against another.... Out of such evaluations will come, I hope, better service to the client. (p. xiii)

The views of Cabot and other historical figures in our field have been taken to heart to such an extent that evaluation studies on the effectiveness of our professional services are now widely seen as the single most significant type of research that social workers can engage in. Table 1 presents a summary of such views.

Table 1: Some Views on the Vital Importance of Evaluation Research in Social Work

- The third type of research, evaluative studies of welfare programs and the activities of practitioners are the most important of all. (Angell, 1954, p. 169)

- Social work, as other professions, must take responsibility for evaluating its training, its practice, and its results. (Preston & Mudd, 1956, p. 39)

- Social work is not a science whose aim is to derive knowledge; it is a technology whose aim is to apply knowledge for the purpose of control. Therefore, on the research continuum, social work research falls nearer to the applied end because of its purpose of practice knowledge. (Greenwood, 1957, p. 315)

- Evaluation and client feedback are not only necessary for effective service delivery, but are an ethical requirement for the profession. Systematic methods must be developed to assess whether social workers are helping, harming, or doing nothing for the people they serve. (Rosenberg & Brody, 1974, p. 349)

- Social work has no more important use of research methods than the assessment of the consequences of practice and policy choices.... Small-scale, agency-based studies are worthwhile if they succeed in placing interest in effectiveness at the center of agency practice and when they create a critical alliance between practitioners and researchers. (Mullen, 1995, pp. 282–283)

- Studies are needed on the effectiveness of psychosocial intervention, including interventions previously tested under ideal controlled conditions in real-world health care systems. (Ell, 1996, p. 589)

- Human service programs no longer have the option of putting off *regular, ongoing, systematic outcomes measurement* [italics in original]. Outcomes measurement systems are now required for organizational, professional, and community survival. . . it means that data must be routinely gathered so that they are readily available for both external accountability and for internal learning and redesign. (Mullen & Magnabosco, 1997a, p. 315)

- Research on actual service interventions is the critical element in connecting research to the knowledge base used by professional practitioners. The issue is now one of developing investigations of social work intervention initiatives: studies that go beyond descriptions and explanatory research. (Austin, 1998, p. 17, 43)

- We need to establish a research agenda in social work. And intervention studies must be high in priority to such an agenda. (Rosen, Proctor, & Staudt, 1999, p. 9)

These are some of the issues that we discuss in this book: how to measure client problems and circumstances in a credible manner, how to determine if clients have improved, and, in some cases, how to determine if they truly got better because of social work services as opposed to simply the passage of time or to placebo influences, and how to find out if the results are long lasting. We will also discuss some of the ethical and pragmatic issues that surround the efforts of social workers to evaluate the outcomes of their own practice or of their agency's programs. And, lastly, we address some common myths and misconceptions that may hinder such work.

For the purposes of our discussion, let's assume that an intervention has been shown to produce results superior to those obtained via nonspecific or nonprofessional care or by a credible placebo. Next, we'd like to see if the new intervention is any better than existing, accepted treatments, and, if so, are the positive effects enduring? A social work intervention that results in improvements lasting only a short period of time is obviously not as helpful to our clientele as one whose beneficial effects last for years and years. This, of course, requires the design and conduct of long-term, follow-up studies. If the new treatment is found to have long-lasting, positive effects, it would also be nice to see if there are any ancillary benefits. For example, an intervention for alcohol abuse might naturally focus on assessing reductions in a client's drinking. This would be a good thing to do, but it would also be nice to know (and demonstrate) that there are collateral improvements in other areas of the client's life, such as in the marital relationship, physical health, or overall quality of life. And, just as medications can be effective yet also result in significant, adverse side effects, so too can psychosocial interventions provided by social workers generate unanticipated, deleterious consequences or so-called iatrogenic effects. Finally, perhaps (if you live long enough), assuming the treatment works well, is better than a placebo or existing services, has long-lived effects, produces positive side effects and no negative ones, one could, in one's old age, begin some sort of study trying to tease out exactly why and how one's treatment works.

By this time, you may want to put this book down, thinking that you could never embark on such a prolonged period of research inquiry. Well, you may be right that you won't do this type of intensive work, but you can take heart in knowing that very few professionals do either (certainly the authors have not). Rather, what most practitioners who choose to undertake evaluation research focus on are the very early stages of this process: namely, trying to find out, with credible data, whether their clients have gotten any better. Few clinical researchers undertake answering the full spectrum of questions one through eight at the beginning of this chapter. The more common model is for someone to address one or more of them, complete and publish a set of investigations, and then have their line of inquiry picked up and built upon by a new set of investigators. This may occur over years or even decades. Examples of this approach can be found in the history of evaluation research in such diverse fields as psychoanalysis, behavior therapy, and pharmacotherapy. In each field, the original investigatory reports progressed from anecdotal case studies to nonblinded preexperiments; then to quasi-experiments, to genuine experiments, and randomized controlled trials; to comparisons with placebos, evaluations of long-term effects, and a dissection of the mechanisms of action.

The metaphor of the relay race comes to mind, with the research baton being passed from one investigator or team on to another over the years. Some team members run long and fast and others only for brief periods or at a slower pace. Meanwhile, constant progress is being made, knowledge advances, and we gain an ever clearer understanding of the effects of a given intervention with the passage of time.

Hawkins and Mathews (1999) have described these initial inquiries into the outcomes of practice as Level 1 research. In Level 1 research, your purpose is not to understand why the clients may have changed, but to adequately document such changes. This does not require the use of a large-group design, control groups, or inferential statistics, but simply the collection of reliable and valid data on client functioning before and after (and perhaps during) social work intervention. The independent variable, the intervention, is whatever of a therapeutic nature the social worker and client agree to undertake together. It can be multifaceted, composed of elements up to and including the proverbial "kitchen sink." Hawkins suggests the following:

> Clinical practice in an office is often done in a manner comparable to driving a car in heavy fog and without a clear destination. Clinicians who neglect to define specific, measurable goals, design and implement plans to reach those goals, measure progress continuously, and graph the data are not providing the best clinical services they can. The retrospective, subjective, global reports on which clinicians often rely are subject to various kinds of error, such as the client's failure to notice important events occurred, forgetting, being unduly influenced by most recent events, being unduly influenced by one or two salient events, attempting to make themselves look better than they really are, and trying to please the clinician. (Hawkins & Mathews, 1999, pp. 124–125)

Sound familiar? It certainly did to us. Hawkins chose to focus on the use of single-system research designs, and, while we will present and illustrate their use, we will also pay considerable attention to applications of designs using larger numbers of clients or group research designs (GRD). Both approaches have their strengths and weaknesses and can be applied in diverse practice settings. Together, these designs represent the most commonly used methodologies in the evaluation of the outcomes of social work practice.

The evaluation of one's own practice has only two prerequisites: (a) locate and obtain one or more credible measures that can be practically applied to assess client functioning, and (b) use such measures repeatedly over time with your client. Everything else in this book is simply a variation on these two themes. In the next chapter, we discuss some ways you can measure the client's functioning or situation and how to develop suitable ways to do this, and, in the succeeding two chapters, we describe the variety of ways these outcome measures can be applied in the contexts of single-system designs (SSDs) and GRDs. We hope that you find this presentation helpful.

2

Selecting and Locating Outcome Measures Useful in the Evaluation of Practice

The topic of selecting and using outcome measures to evaluate your own practice is very congruent with the process described in social work practice as *assessment*. But, given that evaluating practice cuts across the areas of both practice and research, greater attention needs to be given to using outcome measures that are reliable, valid, practical, intelligible, sensitive to meaningful changes, easy to score and interpret, and low in cost in terms of money, time, and other resources. The process of empirically assessing clients, groups, families, organizations, and even larger systems has been given serious attention within professional social work from the very beginnings of our profession. One quite interesting book, perhaps primarily for the sense of historical perspective it provides, but also for some of its substantive content, is Mary Richmond's classic text, *Social Diagnosis*, published in 1917. In it, she makes the case for the crucial importance of careful assessment preceding intervention in social work and that assessment and diagnostic skills (this was not referring to diagnosis in the psychiatric sense so common today) were as important a set of skills as those relating to providing treatment. She provides lengthy discussions of assessing various systems that are the focus of social work treatment (primarily individuals and families) and of the value in seeking out many sources of information from identified clients, their families, relatives, medical doctors, schools, employers, neighbors, social service agencies, and others. She describes gathering data via clinical interviews, letters and surveys, public records, and other documentary sources. She also presents specific assessment approaches for various clientele, such as those who are homeless, disabled, neglected, blind, mentally ill, or intellectually disabled. Richmond lays great strength on gathering not only useful information, but information that is credible, discussing different types of evidence, rules of evidence, and how to make legitimate inferences from such evidence. She went so far as to say:

No considerable group of social case workers . . . seem to have grasped that the *reliability* [italics in original] of the evidence on which they base their decisions should be no less rigorously scrutinized than is that of legal evidence by opposing counsel. (p. 39)

Social evidence differs from legal evidence in that it is more inclusive and that the questions at issue are more complex. For these reasons, careful scrutiny of the reliability of each item of such evidence is all the more necessary. (p. 50)

Over the years, a number of social workers have paid attention to this issue and there are some fine examples of early efforts to develop empirically based outcome measures suitable for use in our practice. Hunt and Kogan's (1952) Movement Scale was one approach to evaluating changes in clients, as was Geismar and Ayers's attempt to identify patterns of social functioning in families (cited in Shyne, 1962).

The closest we have to a contemporary counterpart to Richmond's *Social Diagnosis* is Catheleen Jordan and Cynthia Franklin's (2003) *Clinical Assessment for Social Workers: Quantitative and Qualitative Approaches*, a most useful book that covers a wide array of theoretical and pragmatic approaches to assessment. In this book, they cite the definition of social work assessment as provided by Levine (2002):

The process of systematically collecting data about a client's functioning and monitoring progress in client functioning on an ongoing basis. Assessment is used to identify and measure specific problem behaviors as well as protective and resiliency factors, and to determine if treatment is necessary. (p. 830)

While this is a useful beginning, it omits some other important areas of assessment pertinent to social work practice, as in assessment of families, couples, small groups, organizations, and higher-level systems. It also fails to capture assessment efforts that are related to the design and conduct of outcome studies making use of GRDs, efforts that may not be related to determining a course of treatment (that may have already been decided upon in the research protocol) and may only involve assessment at a very few points in time. But, with these limitations in mind, Levine's definition is a good starting point.

A comprehensive assessment of a client–systems' situation may involve a very large number of domains to examine, but the focus of this chapter shall be on a rather limited aspect of assessment: namely, the selection of one or more outcome measures that can be useful to you in your evaluation of the outcomes of your own practice. We wish to stress the point that assessing client functioning for the purposes of clinical or program evaluation, while a very important piece of social work assessment, is by no means a replacement for the traditional, more comprehensive approach to assessment as illustrated by Richmond (1917), Northen (1987), Mullen and Magnabosco (1997b) or Jordan and Franklin (2003). Nor are generalized assessment models adequate by themselves since some very highly specific approaches to assessment have been developed for use with clients with discrete problems.

For example, if you are undertaking to help a client who meets the *Diagnostic and Statistical Manual of Mental Disorders* (*DSM-IV-TR*; American Psychiatric Association, 2000) criteria for bipolar disorder, you need to be adept not only in using a generic model of social work assessment, but also in using the very highly specific approaches especially developed for practice with this clientele, involving the measuring of mania, depression, medication adherence, drug side effects, and perhaps other aspects, such as caregiver burden, marital issues, and so on (see Clement & Greene, 2002). The same caveat needs to be given for dozens of other specific disorders or problems—you must develop an in-depth knowledge about empirically supported assessment methods specific to unique client problems. If you do not do this, you will be unable to develop a proper understanding of the client-in-situation, and your ability to formulate an effective treatment plan will be accordingly compromised. Solely generic skills in either assessment or treatment are *not* a sufficient foundation for competent social work practice in the 21st century. More specialized skills closely related to specific problems and issues are also required.

WHAT IS ASSESSMENT?

> Many people . . . carry on social investigations—which is the most difficult investigation there is—who don't know how to count. They can't find the recurring social unit that they wish to get the result from. (cited in Claghorn, 1908, p. 251)

This quote illustrates the early recognition within our field of the crucial importance of developing or selecting suitable outcome measures useful in the evaluation of social work practice. In assessing client functioning, you really are limited to three types of information or domains of functioning:

1. Assessment of observable behavior

2. Assessment of client self-reports of behavior, affect, thoughts or perceptions

3. Assessment (in selected domains of practice) of relevant physiological variables

The assessment principle of triangulation is defined as:

> The use of more than one imperfect data-collection alternative in which each option is vulnerable to different potential sources of error. For example, instead of relying exclusively on a client's self-report of how often a particular target behavior occurred during a specified period, a significant other (teacher, cottage parent, and so on) is asked to monitor the behavior as well. (Rubin & Babbie, 2005, p. 758)

It is always a good idea to try to assess a client's situation across two or more aspects of these domains. Think of the folktale of the blind men encountering an elephant. Each thinks the elephant resembles the part of the elephant they themselves have a hold of: the ear, the trunk, the leg, the side, and so on. None of the men is completely on target, but, by correlating more than one aspect, one can end up with a more accurate picture of the elephant. Any number of client problems are manifested across different domains. For example, major depression has behavioral aspects (e.g., sleeping too much, eating too little, weeping a lot, etc.), cognitive elements ("I do not have any hope for the future"), and affective ones ("I feel blue"). Any assessment that does not undertake the measure of all three areas will, by necessity, be incomplete.

Another way of conceptualizing assessment is through the lenses of direct versus indirect assessments. The actual measurement of occurrences of violence directed against a spouse is the most direct way to assess domestic violence, but, unfortunately, social workers do not possess the God-like level of omniscience required for direct appraisal of the client's situation. Therefore, we often rely on indirect measures that may be one or two or more levels removed from the actual core problem. A client's scores on the "Physical" section of the Hudson Partner Abuse Scale (Hudson & McIntosh, 1981) may well be useful, albeit indirect, measures of the occurrence or severity of domestic violence between two partners. But scores on this rapid assessment instrument (RAI) are not isomorphic with measures of actual episodes of violence, which is the real focus of assessment. Asking clients about their current experiences related to hallucinations or delusions is one of the best ways we have of capturing their perceptual experiences, but we should not delude ourselves into thinking we are measuring what a client is experiencing. We are measuring what the client *says* he or she is experiencing, which may be a far cry from what the client is actually perceiving.

Generally speaking, the more direct an approach we have to measuring something the better, and the more aspects or domains we can tap into the better.

The overall perspective of this chapter is as follows:

- If something exists (e.g., a client's problem), it has the potential to be measured.

- If something is credibly measured, then the practitioner is in a better position to more effectively help the client.

- If a client problem/situation can be validly measured, then the social worker is in a better position to see whether the efforts are followed by improvements in the client's life.

One U.S. governor recently asserted, "If you don't measure something, you don't care," justifying his state's use of standardized testing to assess students' learning. While his link between measuring and caring may be extreme, the point is worth stressing that intervention in the absence of careful assessment is likely to be less effective than an interventive plan derived from a careful assessment.

MEASURING OBSERVABLE BEHAVIOR

Many problems experienced by social work clients are manifested through the overt behavior of the client. Sometimes these behaviors are those of commission, for example, drinking too much, being abusive, acting "crazy," and so on, while others are those of omission, for example, not seeking work, failing to engage in proper hygiene, or neglecting children. Direct measures of behavior, assuming they are reliable, usually possess tremendous "face validity," in that it seems reasonable and plausible to assess such obvious aspects of the client's problem, whenever possible.

As outlined in Hudson and Thyer (1987), you have a number of options to assess behavior, such as:

- Client self-monitoring: useful for behaviors that are exclusively private or occur infrequently. This can be done very simply, like keeping track of the number of cigarettes smoked or more formally, using a log, checklist, or diary of some sort.

- Collateral monitoring: wherein the client's behavior is recorded by someone else, such as a spouse, friend, parent, teacher, coworker, or caregiver. This can be informally done or can be more structured, using the aforementioned diaries, logs, or checklists. Collateral monitoring may be undertaken overtly, with the client's awareness and consent or sometimes covertly, without consent or awareness. Careful attention should be given to the ethical proprieties of this latter form of assessment, but it should not be dismissed out of hand as never appropriate.

- Situational tests: involve contrived situations wherein the client is observed while engaging in some activity related to his or her clinical situation. Role-playing exercises, problem-solving tasks, behavioral approach tests (BATs), and so on are examples of situational tests. In a BAT, a person with a phobic condition is asked to come as close as possible to his or her phobic stimulus (e.g., a leashed dog, a caged snake, etc.), while measures of distance, self-reported anxiety, and perhaps heart rate are recorded. BATs can be given before and after treating phobic clients, with successful intervention being associated with the client coming much closer to the phobic stimulus, being more comfortable, and having a slower heart rate posttreatment compared to pretreatment. Curtis and Thyer (1983) and Thyer and Curtis (1983) used this method, which also illustrated the principle of triangulation in measurement in that concurrent measures were taken in all three domains of the client's "phobia:" behavior, self-reported affect, and physiology (heart rate). Situational tests have been widely used in social work with groups, especially with clients seeking to improve interpersonal skills.

- Real-life assessments: unlike situational tests that are contrived, these consist of accompanying clients into the real-world environments, wherein they experience their problems and measuring their behavior. For example, instead of arranging for the client to practice interpersonal skills during a session of group therapy with other clients, the social worker accompanies the client into a real-life setting to observe and later provide feedback.

We hope that you do not find this emphasis on behavior off-putting. We are talking about far more than simply measuring publicly observable actions on the part of clients. We subscribe to the definition of behavior found in *The Social Work Dictionary* (Barker, 2003): "Any action or response by an individual, including observable activity, measurable physiological changes, cognitive images, fantasies, and emotions" (p. 40). Put another way, anything the person does, feels, or thinks is considered behavior: it is what the person does, and this is very often a significant aspect of client functioning and hence worth measuring.

We are also not asserting that the behavior is always the central problem or that it is the only aspect of the client's situation that is important. We are not. But sometimes the behaviors themselves are very important indeed and can be the most distressing aspect of the client's situation. Practitioners of every theoretical persuasion agree that behavior change is an important aspect of social work intervention, and our laying some stress on this does not imply we suggest that behavior change is the only relevant indicator of therapeutic progress. Sometimes, many times, environmental change is the most useful measure of improvement, and, in some circumstances, changes in emotional development, personal strengths, one's capacity to love, to forgive, or to overcome, can all be significant elements of the definition of success. Even Anna

Freud, daughter of Sigmund Freud and a widely regarded psychotherapist in her own right, operating from the perspective of psychoanalytic theory, noted that "The analyst as behaviorist can use pieces of behavior to infer for example how a child deals with anxiety or frustration" (cited in Gregory, 1987, p. 71). The distinguished social worker Gordon Hamilton (1940) provided a similar rationale: "If it is true that behavior is purposive, then how the individual behaves is at least one key to understanding him, even in a complex situation" (p. 27).

Another well-known social work educator and theorist, Carol H. Meyer (1973), stated it this way:

> The apparent purpose of these practice approaches is to change behaviors, attitudes, coping mechanisms, perceptions and feelings of clients . . . the essential purpose is change in the client himself. (p. 95)

While we believe that Meyer gives insufficient attention in this passage to the issue of environmental modification as an important outcome for some types of social work practice, you can see through these quotations how behavior change is viewed as one important benefit of our professional services.

There is a role for some parsimony in description however. Take the observation of the prescient Mary Richmond (1917): "To say that we think our client is mentally deranged is futile; to state the observations that have created this impression is a possible help" (p. 335), and the later, but similar, recommendation of Helen Northen (1987): "The problem should be based on facts, not inferences, and it should be defined in operational terms" (p. 175).

To better illustrate this, Bruce Thyer is standing in front of his class and there is slight tremor in his hands. It would be a violation of the principle of parsimony for a student to observe that Bruce is nervous. That would be an inference, a conclusion from a more fundamental observation, and this conclusion may or may not be true. Given the limited data, there is no way to tell. But might it be that Bruce has had too much hot tea to drink that morning and is overloaded on caffeine? Or has he not eaten anything for some time and is hypoglycemic, with the low blood sugar causing the tremor? Perhaps he has taken a medication containing pseudoephedrine, a stimulant that can cause tremors? It is far more appropriate to limit oneself to facts one can directly observe and to what people do or say than to omit this foundational information in lieu of presenting one's inferences, filtered through the screen of your own perspectives or theoretical lens.

The quote above by Helen Northen introduces the idea of an operational definition to the assessment process, defined as "the explanation of the phenomenon to be studied in terms of how it will be measured" (Barker, 2003, p. 306) and "the concrete and specific definition of something in terms of the operations by which observations are to be categorized" (Rubin & Babbie, 2005, p. 752). Deciding *what* and *how* you choose to measure something is coming up with your operational definition of your outcome measure. A client's scores on the Beck Depression Inventory might be one outcome measure in a study evaluating the effects of psychosocial treatment of depression. Numbers of days living in the community, perhaps combined with some measure of employment, might be useful outcome measures for a program of assertive community treatment for individuals with chronic mental illness. A child's school attendance can be operationally defined by the school's official attendance records, and a juvenile court's success can be defined in terms of the recidivism rates of youths adjudicated through that court.

If you pick a poor outcome measure, then your study will be of little value no matter how competently carried out, hence the importance of knowing how to locate and use good quality indicators.

Polster and Collins (1993) provide a dated, but high-quality overview of using structured observations in evaluating clinical practice and larger-scale programmatic outcomes and discuss ways to ensure that your observations are reliable. Apart from simply measuring the frequency (e.g., number of seizures or bed-wetting episodes) with which a behavior occurs, in some cases it may be appropriate to measure other aspects, such as duration (e.g., length of a binge or crying episode, time engaged in working on a productive task, etc.) or magnitude (e.g., numbers of beers consumed, blood alcohol level, etc.). The determination of what approach to measuring behavior is the best is a function of the nature of the problem; practicality; available resources of time, money, and people; and other factors. Baer, Harrison, Fradenburg, Petersen, & Milla (2005) provide a more up-to-date review on methods of measuring behavior, and there are several specialized journals that focus on this area (e.g., *Behavioral Assessment* and *Journal of Psychopathology & Behavioral Assessment*).

RAPID ASSESSMENT INSTRUMENTS

RAIs are client-completed, self-report scales that are also relatively brief, easy for clients to understand and complete, and easy for the clinician to score and interpret. They are most often developed around some central construct, usually a problem, but many assess strengths as well. Most RAIs are scored by summing a client's responses to each question (usually answered using a simple numbering system as in 1=not at all, 2=sometimes, 3=much of the time, etc.), and perhaps reverse scoring some items (a technique used to help ensure that the client puts some thought into marking his or her responses). Usually a single number is arrived at, with higher scores indicating more of whatever the issue is being assessed by that particular RAI. Figure 2.1 illustrates a sample RAI, called the Clinical Anxiety Scale (CAS), developed by one of the authors (Westhuis & Thyer, 1989). This instrument was developed for use in the assessment of clients who meet the *DSM* criteria for severe anxiety disorders such as panic disorder or agoraphobia. Higher scores indicate more serious problems with clinical anxiety, and pilot testing of the RAI involving individuals known to be diagnosed with panic disorder or agoraphobia versus individuals with no history of a serious anxiety disorder found that most of the former scored above 30, while most of the latter scored below 30, hence 30 points is suggested as a clinical cutting score. The CAS has been used as an outcome measure in group evaluation studies (e.g., Valentine & Smith, 2001) and in the evaluation of treatment with individuals (e.g., Maxwell, 2003, Myers, 1997) and is a good example of a measure that can be used as an adjunct to the social worker's clinical judgment, subjective impressions, observations of behavior, and client self-reports in terms of evaluating outcomes.

How can you find instruments like the CAS or other RAIs? Well, the single best resource we recommend is the two-volume *Measures for Clinical Practice: A Sourcebook*, edited by the distinguished academic team of Joel Fischer and Kevin Corcoran (2007). One volume contains information on RAIs useful in practice with adult clients, and the other deals with RAIs that address problems of children, couples, and families. Literally

Figure 2.1

 CLINICAL ANXIETY SCALE (CAS)

Name: _____ Today's Date: _____

This questionnaire is designed to measure how much anxiety you are currently feeling. It is not a test, so there are no right or wrong answers. Answer each item as carefully and as accurately as you can by placing a number beside each one as follows.

1 Rarely or none of the time
2 A little of the time
3 Some of the time
4 A good part of the time
5 Most or all of the time

---

1. ____ I feel calm.
2. ____ I feel tense.
3. ____ I feel suddenly scared for no reason.
4. ____ I feel nervous.
5. ____ I use tranquilizers or antidepressants to cope with my anxiety.
6. ____ I feel confident about the future.
7. ____ I am free from senseless or unpleasant thoughts.
8. ____ I feel afraid to go out of my house alone.
9. ____ I feel relaxed and in control of myself.
10. ____ I have spells of terror or panic.
11. ____ I feel afraid in open spaces or in the streets.
12. ____ I feel afraid I will faint in public.
13. ____ I am comfortable traveling on buses, subways or trains.
14. ____ I feel nervousness or shakiness inside.
15. ____ I feel comfortable in crowds, such as shopping or at a movie.
16. ____ I feel comfortable when I am left alone.
17. ____ I feel afraid without good reason.
18. ____ Due to my fears, I unreasonably avoid certain animals, objects or situations.
19. ____ I get upset easily or feel panicky unexpectedly.
20. ____ My hands, arms or legs shake or tremble.
21. ____ Due to my fears, I avoid social situations, whenever possible.
22. ____ I experience sudden attacks of panic which catch me by surprise.
23. ____ I feel generally anxious.
24. ____ I am bothered by dizzy spells.
25. ____ Due to my fears, I avoid being alone, whenever possible.

1, 6, 7, 9, 13, 15, 16.

hundreds of RAIs are contained therein, and virtually any clinical issue you might encounter in practice will have one or more convenient measures reproduced, along with citations to primary references and scoring and interpretation instructions.

Another very useful resource is the collection of RAIs developed by social worker Walter Hudson and his colleagues. These are commercially available instruments (see http://www.walmyr.com), and most have been examined for their reliability and validity and have subsequently been published in peer-reviewed journals. Sample copies and scoring information can be reviewed on this Web site, and they can be ordered here as well. Over 35 RAIs deal with personal issues (e.g., depression, drug involvement, alcohol use), couples issues (e.g., marital satisfaction, physical abuse, sexual satisfaction), family problems (e.g., family relations, parental attitudes, etc.), and organizational variables (e.g., job satisfaction, managerial effectiveness, etc.).

Some specialized books focus on presenting RAIs dealing with one central construct, such as the volume titled *Practitioners' Guide to Empirically Based Measures of Depression* (Nezu, Ronan, Meadows, & McClure, (2000). The Association for the Advancement of Behavioral and Cognitive Therapies (AABCT) has also sponsored two similar volumes, one presenting empirically based measures of anxiety and the other on measuring school-related behaviors of children. All three volumes may be ordered through the organization's Web site, http://www.aabt.org, and if your practice focuses on any one of these three domains, these particular books represent the very best assessment resources available to you.

The authoritative *Social Worker's Desk Reference* (Roberts & Greene, 2002) is another useful resource for learning about specific assessment approaches, with individual chapters dealing with topics such as crisis assessment, selecting and using assessment tools for use with children, troubled adolescents, families, and one on the important topic of assessing client strengths. Some social work research texts also devote entire chapters to locating and evaluating assessment instruments useful in clinical and program evaluation. Royse et al. (2006) have one fine chapter on this topic and one that reprints a number of selected RAIs representing some common client problems, such as self-esteem, parenting skills, child abuse, and anxiety. Bloom, Fischer, and Orme (2006) provide perhaps the most exhaustive treatment on assessment methods for use in single-subject research designs and is also highly recommended.

We wish to stress that the use by social workers of RAIs does not involve the formal testing of a client's personality or intelligence, domains often reserved by state statute as falling within the scope of practice of licensed psychologists. Rather, applying RAIs, measuring behavior, and assessing selected physiological indices are part and parcel of legitimate social work practice related to the assessment functions of our profession. Richmond (1917) included many examples of structured and semistructured interviews and questionnaires specific for use with clients with particular problems that can be seen as the precursors to today's RAIs. Furthermore, in many instances, social workers themselves have developed, tested, and disseminated RAIs for use in the evaluation of the outcomes of social work practice. These assessment instruments have been published in disciplinary social work journals. The bimonthly professional journal *Research on Social Work Practice,* for example, regularly publishes validation studies on new and existing RAIs, and, over the past 17 years, many dozens of such studies have appeared in this one journal alone.

A rather specialized form of an RAI is called a *Self-Anchored Rating Scale,* also known as *Individualized Rating Scales* (IRSs). These are simple, easy to understand, and use ways to measure the intensity, magnitude, severity, or some other dimension or a construct that is the focus of social work intervention. These are especially useful when no standardized RAI is available to you to use as an outcome measure. IRSs are also useful as supplements to RAIs and can even be used as the sole means of evaluating outcomes (although we do not recommend this because of their unknown reliability and validity—see below).

You can begin by working with the client to help him or her clearly describe what the two of you will be focusing on in treatment. If it is some sort of observable behavior, then directly measuring this would be the way to go. But, if the issue is an internal state of the client or a feeling, for example, creating an IRS with the client may really help you in your assessment efforts and in evaluating outcomes. Begin by jointly selecting with the client what you are going to try to assess. With a client who is clinically depressed, you can draw out a simple horizontal line on a piece of paper or on a computer and label it "depression." Next, divide this line into an odd number of segments, say five, seven, or nine. Label these with numbers and adjectives appropriate to the construct being measured, as in:

No Depression			Severe Depression	
1	2	3	4	5

Clients are then asked to rate themselves on this scale by circling the most appropriate number or by making a tic mark on the line. This can be done, say, once a week during office consultations, perhaps daily by the client, or even more often. If the clients bring these IRSs to their visits with you, then when you ask something like, "How was your depression this week?" Not only can they provide you with the typical, clinically rich narrative description, but also with a series of numbers reflecting a whole week's worth of ratings. These may well prove to be a more accurate depiction of the ebb and flow of depressed affect during the week than the clients' narrative alone.

The following is an example of an IRS for use with a client who experiences pedophiliac urges:

No Urges			Moderate Urges			Very Strong Urges		
1	2	3	4	5	6	7	8	9

You can forego the line altogether, and simply present a rating scale, as in Degree of Irritation with Children.

1	2	3	4	5
No Irritation		Moderate Irritation		Extreme Irritation

The simplest IRSs measure one thing, not two. For example, it makes things easier by measuring irritation with children (as in the above example) than to have "Irritation with Children" at one end of the scale and, say, its opposite "Contentment with Children" on the other end.

One of the earliest examples of an individualized rating scale was developed in the late 1950s by the psychiatrist Joseph Wolpe (1958), who asked clients to rate their anxiety on a zero to 100-point scale with zero being completely relaxed and 100 being the state of sheer panic. This simple measure has been widely used in clinical practice and as an outcome measure in psychotherapy research for many years up to the present. While seemingly simplistic, this measure has been shown to correlate modestly well with various measures of concurrent physiological arousal such as heart rate and finger temperature (Thyer, Papsdorf, Davis & Vallecorsa, 1984; Thyer, Papsdorf, & Wright, 1984). So, these simple little scales that can be constructed by practitioners may prove to have great utility. Bloom et al. (2006) have an entire chapter devoted to this topic and is recommended for a more in-depth review.

PHYSIOLOGICAL MEASURES

Under select circumstances, with clients with certain problems, social workers may make use of assessing certain physiological measures relevant to the client's problem. For example, in assessing the severity of clients' phobia reactions to anxiety-evoking situations, a specialized form of situational test, a BAT, was used before, during, and after psychosocial treatment. During these brief, structured encounters (done with the client's informed consent, of course), in addition to talking with and observing the client, concurrent measures were taken of the client's heart rate, using a simple meter that clipped on to the client's finger. The theory (verified in practice) is that before treatment, clients will have very high heart rates when they are in the vicinity of their phobic stimulus (e.g., a dog, snake, etc.), and, some sessions later, when treatment has been successfully concluded, a repetition of the BAT will find little or no elevations in heart rate during an identical, structured exposure experience.

Some social workers (e.g. Lawrence, Wodarski, & Wodarski, 2002; Thyer et al., 1981) use as a part of their practice the method known as *biofeedback* (called by some *neurofeedback*). Sensors are attached to the skin and measure selected physiological indices such as heart rate, blood pressure, skin conductance, skin temperature, muscle tension, and brain waves. Immediate feedback in the form of sounds, lights, or instrument indicators can be provided or fed back to the client who can learn what to do to reduce muscle tension, skin conductance, and other measures associated with being tense and to enhance skin temperature or the amount of alpha waves produced by the brain, which are measures associated with being more relaxed. The devices attached to the skin (called transducers) are all noninvasive and harmless, and various training and certification programs related to becoming competent in the provision of biofeedback are widely advertised.

In the field of drug and alcohol abuse counseling, it is not uncommon for social workers to be involved in getting the results of urine screens, breathalyzer tests, or assays of the client's hair—all physiological assessment methods that can provide reliable information about recent (and, in some cases, long ago) substance use. Low-cost urine tests that screen for the most commonly abused drugs are now available over the counter at drugstores. The regular, random use of such screens is widely recommended as an important indicator of drug or alcohol use and, when combined with client self-reports, clinical observations, and information from significant others, can provide the social worker with a far more comprehensive assessment of the true state of the client's substance abuse than less formal appraisals (e.g., the clinical interview alone). Many drug treatment programs now use drug screens as an important outcome measure for the success of such programs.

Social workers in selected health care settings may have access to and monitor, along with clients, other physiological measures such as blood sugar tests in helping diabetic patients adhere to their health care regimens of diet and exercise. The frequent and routine monitoring of blood pressure at clinics by staff and at home by clients themselves can be an important source of data for clients seeking treatment for hypertension (high blood pressure), with such information being regularly reviewed with clients by the medical social worker. These variables too can serve as information for pre- and posttreatment measures of outcome and as repeated measures for evaluating practice with individual clients.

RELIABILITY OF MEASUREMENT

By reliability, we mean that an assessment method possesses several desirable features that are essential if it is to be confidently relied upon. If an assessment method is reliable, then it has the potential for being useful. If it is not reliable, then it is not really worth considering any further. Reliability has several different dimensions, and these may vary somewhat across different ways of measuring. Perhaps most fundamentally is the idea that if the client and his or her problem or situation does not really change, then repeated administrations of the assessment method should yield very similar findings. For example, if a client provides a urine sample just prior to an appointment and the results are positive (indicating the recent use of some particular drug), if the test is repeated after the appointment, say an hour later with the same or even a fresh sample of urine, the same result should be forthcoming. If it is not, you may have a test that is so unreliable that you cannot trust the results. If a client completes an RAI assessing some construct, say, depression, and he or she achieves a certain score, and if some time passes (say, a week or two), and the client's depression is really pretty much the same, then, if the client completes the same RAI a second time, the second score should be pretty close to the first score.

Imagine you weigh yourself on the bathroom scale and find that you weigh 130 pounds. You then go and brush your teeth, do nothing else, and, upon stepping on the scale three minutes later again you find you have lost five pounds. While you might be very happy with this result, the chances are the missing five pounds are more because of an unreliable scale than a miracle toothpaste that caused you to lose weight suddenly. This type of reliability, whether the information is obtained from client self-report using an RAI, a mechanical device like a scale, or a chemical analysis like a drug screen, is called test-retest reliability. You should carefully read up on whatever assessment method you are considering adopting as an outcome measure for clinical or program evaluation purposes and see if it has had acceptable test-retest reliability demonstrated. Thyer & Westhuis (1989) is an example of one such report examining the test-retest reliability of an RAI.

Another form of reliability is related to the internal consistency of a measure and usually is relevant when considering RAIs and other formal measures of psychosocial functioning that presumably assess only one major construct. For example, what statement seems to be out of place in the following series:

1. I generally feel blue most of the time.

2. I have trouble falling asleep at night.

3. I am tired most of the time.

4. I love to read about social work research.

5. I worry about the future a great deal.

Hmmmm. . . It should be obvious that statement 4 is the one out of place. Can you guess what construct the other items might be assessing? Yes, depression. For an RAI or other assessment method to possess acceptable internal consistency, it should generally focus on one thing, as items 1, 2, 3, and 5 do in the above example. An RAI that had some of these relevant items, but a fair sprinkling of pretty irrelevant ones, would, when examined, mathematically turn out to have fairly low internal consistency. This type of reliability (internal consistency) is usually assessed with a statistical test called Cronbach's coefficient alpha, a value that can range from 0.00 to 1.00. Generally, you would like to use as an outcome measure for your evaluation efforts an RAI that has a coefficient alpha of .80 or higher for a group outcome study and maybe even .90 if you were using it in the context of a single-subject study. But these are merely estimated guidelines, not hard and fast rules.

Sometimes, RAIs and other assessment methods are intentionally designed to assess several different variables or factors related to a larger construct. For example, a measure of depression might have some items that assess the so-called cognitive aspects of depression (what depressed folks say they think or worry about), as well as the affective (what depressed people say they are feeling) and behavioral (what depressed folks say they are doing or not doing related to sleeping, eating, sexual activity, weeping, etc.) features. In such instances, each subscale or factor on an RAI should have acceptable internal consistency, and an overall alpha coefficient may not be relevant. Some social work journals regularly publish reports on the internal consistency of assessment methods. For example, the May 2006 issue of *Research on Social Work Practice* (see http://rsw.sagepub.com) contained articles about the development, reliability, and validity testing of measures for constructs such as the urban hassles experienced by minority youths, adolescent emotional and behavioral functioning, and the emotional stability of children. Articles such as these should constitute the primary sources for social workers seeking information about the reliability and validity of potential assessment methods.

Another form of reliability is called *interrater reliability* and refers to two or more social workers using a given assessment method and independently coming up with results that are very similar. Adequate interrater reliability is a fundamental property of acceptable assessment instruments. One of the reasons many mental health professionals have reservations about the value of the *DSM* assessment system is that formal tests of the interrater reliabilities of these various sets of diagnostic criteria are either absent or, in some cases, have demonstrated unacceptably low agreement between two judges. Interrater reliability is not conceptually difficult to understand. If social worker number one interviews a client, say Sherlock Holmes (a known user of cocaine via injection) and concludes that Mr. Holmes meets the *DSM* criteria for cocaine abuse, one would hope that social worker number 2, who separately assesses Mr. Holmes later than day, would arrive at the same diagnosis and, of course, be able to do so while in ignorance of social worker number one's assessment. To the extent that this is demonstrated across a wide array of cocaine abusers and clinicians, then the interrater reliability of the *DSM*'s diagnostic criteria for cocaine abuse can be said to have been established. Social worker Stuart Kirk has been one of the foremost critics of the *DSM* system of assessing presumptive psychopathology, in large part because of the *unreliability* that is evident for many of the disorders listed within the *DSM* (see Hseih & Kirk, 2005, for one recent critical analysis).

VALIDITY IN MEASUREMENT

An RAI, a structured clinical interview, a situational test, a measure of physiological functioning, or any other form of social work assessment should possess another quality besides being reliable. It must also be valid. Validity has been described as follows:

> A descriptive term used of a measure that accurately reflects the concept that it is intended to measure. For example, your IQ would seem a more *valid* measure of your intelligence than the number of hours you spend in the library. Realize that the ultimate *validity* of a measure can never be proven, but we may still agree to its relative *validity, content validity, construct validity, internal validation,* and *external validation.* This must not be confused with reliability. (Rubin & Babbie, 2005, p. 758)

A simpler definition is presented by Barker (2003): "The concept concerned with the extent to which a procedure is able to measure the quality it is intended to measure" (p. 453).

The easiest concept to grasp related to validity is the idea of face validity, a subjective judgment on the part of professionals that a given approach to measurement is actually capturing what it is supposed to be measuring. Here is a more formal definition of face validity:

> A test is assumed to be valid for the prediction of an external criterion if the terms which compose it "appear on their face" to bear a common-sense relationship with the objective of the test. The assumption of validity in this case is asserted to be so strong that statistical evidence of validity of unnecessary. (Mosier, 1947, p. 192)

Usually, the more direct a measure is, the greater is its face validity. Take, for example, the concept of drug abuse. Were it possible to directly observe each and every instance of the occurrence of drug ingestion on the part of a client, along with the quantity of drugs consumed and the duration of a period of drug use, such behavioral observations would have pretty good face validity. A less direct measure would be periodic but random drug screens (e.g., urinalysis). An even less direct measure would be the client's self-report on an RAI, such as his or her score on Walter Hudson's *Index of Drug Involvement* (IDI, Faul & Hudson, 1997).

The IDI consists of 25 questions to be answered on a 1 (none of the time) to 7 (all of the time) scale and includes items such as "I feel that I use too much drugs," "When I do use drugs, I get into fights," "I use drugs several times a week," and so on. All these approaches would been generally seen as having good face validity, with most professionals in the field agreeing that these ways of assessing drug abuse are pretty much on target. Contrast this with some considerably less direct methods of assessment such as projective tests used by some psychologists—the Rorschach inkblot test or the thematic apperception test—wherein clients verbalize what they see in ink blots or tell stories about a set of structured pictures (e.g., Gordon, 1980). These tests would seem to have little surface connection to a given client's drug abuse and accordingly be seen as having minimal face validity.

Content validity involves a determination of the extent to which a measure adequately samples the full range of phenomena associated with a given construct. Let's take the common problem of clinical depression. Depression may be viewed as potentially manifesting itself in at least three aspects or domains: those pertaining to overt behavior, those pertaining to the client's affect, and those relating to the client's thinking. Behaviorally, depression may touch upon one's sleeping, eating, or sexual functioning. Frequent weeping is one common behavior found among the depressed. In terms of affect, clients usually say that they feel blue, blah, depressed, down in the dumps, tired, have little appetite, and so forth. And, in terms of thoughts, they may say they are preoccupied with thoughts of suicide, how to do away with themselves, are worried about the future, ruminate over the past, or say that they believe things are hopeless, will never improve, and that there is no point in continuing. In order for a given measure of "depression" to have adequate content validity, it must satisfactorily assess all three of these discrete areas. If a measure only looked at, say, the behavioral aspects alone, the affective alone, or the cognitive alone, that measure would not have good construct validity as it would be only a partial measure of the concept in question.

The disorder called schizophrenia is commonly said to have two types of symptoms, positive and negative ones. The positive symptoms of schizophrenia involve what such people do or a distortion of normal functions, such as delusions, hallucinations, bizarre speech, or other behavior (like wearing six sweaters at once during the hot summer). Negative symptoms involve more of what people don't do, as in restricted speech, failure to engage in appropriate personal hygiene or to interact socially, the display of flattened affect, failure to work, and so forth. Any measure of schizophrenia that purports to be a comprehensive measure needs to adequately address both the positive and negative symptoms. For example, the Brief Psychiatric Rating Scale is one commonly used system for clinicians to rate the symptoms of serious mental illness of clients. It assesses various positive (e.g., hallucinations, motor hyperactivity, mannerisms, and posturing) and negative symptoms (e.g., self-neglect, blunted affect, and motor retardation). A measure of schizophrenia that only addressed one aspect, say, positive symptoms, would not be considered to have adequate content validity for the overall phenomenon we have labeled "schizophrenia."

Take the measurement of insomnia, for example. If one were developing a client-completed rapid assessment scale or a simple of set of questions that addressed only the amount of time it takes one to fall asleep, this would neglect other aspects of the problem labeled "insomnia," such as early-morning wakening or intermittent waking throughout the night. A client with insomnia could be troubled by one, two, or all three aspects of troubled sleep, and any measure that failed to assess all these relevant dimensions would be judged to have low content validity.

In summary, content validity refers to the adequacy or comprehensiveness by which a given measure addresses the assessment of a particular construct. The appraisal of content validity is a subjective judgment by presumptive experts in the area (which may include clients themselves, of course) and a qualitative judgment as opposed to a quantitative characteristic of a measurement, such as internal consistency or interrater agreement. Any outcome measure that seems to lack adequate content validity is usually a poor choice for use in evaluating practice outcomes.

Concurrent validity refers to the extent that a given measure correlates well with other valid indices of a client's problem or functioning. Do scores on a diagnostic rating scale correlate highly with expert clinician's diagnostic assessments? If so, the measure can be said to have good concurrent validity. This was the approach used by Dan Mosley, a social worker with a forensic facility at Fulton State Hospital in Missouri in his efforts to see if the Forensic Competency Scale he developed was valid (see Mosley, Thyer, & Larrison, 2001). Dan gave his 21-item, true-false RAI to 75 mentally ill prisoners up for a forensic competency hearing. *Forensic competency* is another term for sanity and reflects the prisoner's ability to understand the legal proceedings and to participate in the prisoner's own defense. The true-false items included statements such as "I cannot ever change attorneys" and "Not guilty means that I committed the offense." Dan then compared scores on this measure with a forensic psychologist's later determination of the prisoner's competency and the later determination of the court regarding the prisoner's competency. These later determinations were made without knowledge of the prisoner's score on Dan's scale. Using a cutting score of 17 (saying that those who scored 17 or above were competent) produced the best results, in that with such a cutting score, Dan's RAI results agreed with those of the forensic psychologist 75% of the time and with the court's determination 76% of the time. This level of agreement is statistically higher than chance and suggests that the Mosley Forensic Competency Scale can be useful in the initial appraisal of a prisoner's sanity in a legal sense.

Now, of course, it would be better for Dan's scale to agree with the psychologist's and court's determinations 100% of the time, but such high levels of concurrent validity are very rare for any measure.

Discriminant validity consists of the extent to which a given measure is capable of distinguishing individuals with a problem from those without it. The most common way to test a new scale is by administering it to two groups of people—those with the problem and those without—and seeing if their scores are sufficiently disparate. The more overlap in the scores between the two groups, the less useful the measure may be. The less overlap, the better in terms of discriminant validity. The logic is somewhat simplistic. If people known to have a problem, say, major depression, usually score above a certain level on an RAI, while folks known to not be depressed usually score below that level, the score of your client who completes the RAI may suggest whether he or she is more like individuals who are clinically depressed versus those who are not depressed. Now, to be sure, such scores should not be considered to be definitively diagnostic. There are always individual differences, subtleties in how a given client interprets the content of a scale, and often the range of scores between groups of folks with and without a problem overlaps somewhat, which can complicate the interpretation of a given score. Nevertheless, using RAIs that have been shown to reliably and validly distinguish between people with a given problem from those who do not is certainly preferable to using RAIs that lack known discriminant validity.

Most of the scales found in the sources mentioned in this chapter have been found to possess sufficiently satisfactory reliability and validity and can be considered for use in the valuation of the outcomes of social work practice. However, new research is always being undertaken on these and newer measures, so a review of recent developments in the literature using a comprehensive electronic database such as *PsycInfo* at your local college or university library is always a good idea.

AVOID WEAK, INVALID, OR BOGUS ASSESSMENT METHODS

There is a form of treatment called thought field therapy (you can Google this phrase to learn more about TFT) and, among its claims, are that a properly trained TFT practitioner can listen to you on the telephone and, from the sound of your voice, diagnose which spots on your body should be systematically tapped in a prescribed way to effect a cure for whatever mental or emotional disorder ails you. We are not making this up. Moreover, if you should wish to learn how to practice this amazing therapy, you must pay a fee of $100,000 to the inventor of this technique for a three-day, one-on-one training session. An entire issue of a respected journal, *Journal of Clinical Psychology,* was devoted to original studies, critical commentary, and responses on TFT, and nonskeptical social workers might think there is something legitimate about this form of assessment and treatment. According to the Thought Field Therapy 4U Web site (http://www.tft4u. co.uk/page2.htm), TFT is predicated on the idea that thinking about your problem and then being instructed to tap with your fingertip various so-called meridian areas on your body (e.g., eyebrow, collarbone, and the back of the hands). The Web site claims that TFT:

> Has the capability of DISABLING and often completely ELIMI-NATING troublesome emotional and physical responses. . . Simple problems can be solved within minutes, while more complex problems such as trauma, acute anxiety, depression, addictive urge may require further investigation over two or three sessions.

How does this work?

> In TFT we are using those meridian points in much same way as a computer operator might use a PC keyboard—as a means of inputting coded instruction. . . by stimulating these points in the correct order we are able to deactivate the perturbation. In other words, by tapping in the necessary code, we appear to be supplying the mind with a "delete" instruction. . . The negative response has been switched off and is no longer there!

Suffice it to say that these meridian points on your body, supposedly corresponding to points used in acupuncture, have never been shown to exist as any kind of a "switch" or nexus of invisible energies of the body and are otherwise unknown to mainstream science. And we can be pretty sure that any benefits of TFT or the assessment approach called voice technology are primarily derived from placebo influences. How do we know that? Because of the excellent randomized controlled study of TFT conducted by a licensed social worker, Monica Pignotti (2004, 2005a, 2005b, 2005c), who had been properly trained in TFT. Supposedly, the therapist's assessment of the client reveals which meridian points require proper tapping, in what sequence and frequency. According to the proponents of TFT, it is seen as crucial that the proper switches are chosen and tapped correctly. What Monica did was to treat a large series of patients with TFT and randomly assigned half of them to be treated with real TFT, using the proper meridian points and sequencing of taps called for this approach, and the other half received superficially the same treatment. But, unbeknownst to them, the meridian points and tapping sequences were chosen *randomly*. The first group, those who received legitimate TFT, reported improvements. However, the clients who received pseudo-TFT reported *equivalent improvements*. This crucial study by a social worker provided a long-overdue and important test of the central premises of the assessment and treatment protocols of TFT and seemed to convincingly demonstrate that these premises are false (see Pignotti, 2004, 2005a, 2005b, 2005c; see also Waite & Holder, 2003). We mention this to you to illustrate that there are a number of assessment methods floating around, offered commercially, written about in our textbooks, taught in our BSW and MSW classrooms, and conveyed through our approved continuing education courses: methods that are most charitably conceived as misguided and more harshly viewed as bogus, as flimflam, or outright fraudulent.

Radionics, for example, involves a therapist holding a pendulum over a client and asking the pendulum questions about presumptive illnesses, disorders, or diagnostic issues. How the pendulum swings (e.g., back and forth, up and down, or in a circle or oval) provides the answer to questions. This, of course, is bogus, but training in radionics was advertised in the monthly newsletter of the American Psychological Association (APA) a few years ago. You can Google "radionics" to learn more about this bogus method of assessment.

You may have run across the term *facilitated communication* (FC). This is an approach to the assessment of the intelligence of individuals with severe intellectual disabilities. In FC, a "facilitator" sits next to a client in front of a computer screen and keypad. The client's hand is formed into a fist with the index finger extended, and the facilitator gently holds the client's hand while moving it back and forth across the keyboard. The client is asked a question and appears to type out answers. Now keep in mind these are clients who do not speak and have never been taught the alphabet nor the rudiments of grammar, yet, through the use of FC, it makes it look as if they are far more aware of events in their lives than they were before, and, using this technique, they are capable of holding sustained conversations with their parents, caregivers, and others. This seemed to represent a genuine breakthrough in the assessment and treatment of people with severe intellectual disabilities (e.g., mental retardation, autistic disorder, etc.) and generated considerable enthusiasm in the community of parents and care providers for persons with developmental disabilities. Expensive training sessions were offered so that people could become officially qualified facilitated communicators, and such workshops were provided across the country. Parents began demanding this technique for their child and were amazed at the hidden depths of intelligence FC appeared to reveal. Worthy of note is that the proponents of FC and those trained in the technique swore up and down that they were not guiding the client's answers and that they were merely supporting the hand. It sounded too good to be true. And it was.

Some clever researchers set up the following test: A client and his FC wore headphones. The researcher asked a question, and both client and facilitator heard it: for example, "Allen, what did you have for breakfast today?" And Allen would peck out an appropriate answer. This would be repeated a number of times. Then a question would be posed at the same time over the headphones, but the questions were *different*: the client heard one question, and the facilitator heard another. The answers that subsequently emerged related to the question heard by the facilitator, not the client. A series of elegantly simple tests like this, repeated with many different clients and properly trained facilitators, revealed the same result. It appears that, all along, the facilitators were unknowingly guiding the client's hands in answering the questions. It now seems that FC was nothing more than an elaborate Ouija-board phenomenon. Think of the waste in hundreds of social workers and other mental health professionals going to the expense and trouble of becoming certified in FC. Think of the falsely elevated hopes, the elation, and then the crushing deflation experienced by the caregivers and parents of severely disabled people who pursued FC in good faith, persuaded perhaps by the "credentials" and academic degrees of this technique's proponents (see Green & Shane, 1994; Jacobson, Foxx, & Mulick, 2005).

Other examples of controversial and questionable assessment techniques used in social work and other human services include methods such as using anatomically correct dolls with children to assess presumptive sexual abuse; hypnosis to help clients uncover so-called repressed memories of childhood sexual abuse; the Rorschach inkblot test, the thematic apperception test, or client drawings of human beings, houses, or trees (these latter three methods usually administered by psychologists, but sometimes used by social workers); and the Myers-Briggs Type Indicator, a presumptive measure of personality, recently recommended for use in helping social work faculty place students in field instruction placements (Moore, Dettlaff, & Dietz, 2004). Extensive research on all these assessment methods has failed to demonstrate their reliability and validity, and, in most cases, the underlying theory is clearly erroneous. Lilienfeld, Lynn, and Lohr (2003) provide a very interesting and informative overview of such pseudoscientific assessment methods in the mental health and health care arenas.

Whenever you consider learning about some assessment methods, the proper attitude is that of scientific skepticism—not an *a priori* denial of the usefulness of the method, but rather the professionally legitimate request to be provided with credible evidence that the method is both reliable and valid. Genuine professionals do not uncritically adopt new methods simply because some authority figure (supervisor, field instructor, faculty member, agency director, etc.) says they should. Rather, express an interest in learning more about the method and request references to articles published in credible professional journals that have examined these new methods of assessment. If this became a widespread practice, we would see far fewer unjustified fads in our field and less exposure of hapless clients to ineffective methods of assessment.

BIAS IN USING VARIOUS ASSESSMENT METHODS

It is important to remember that although a social worker has succeeded in obtaining some quantifiable measures related to client functioning used in assessing outcomes, the information obtained may be biased or distorted in various ways. For example, using printed RAIs or IRSs with clients whose native language is not English may pose problems. Sure, they may mark items on a page or pick a number to rate themselves on some construct, but their genuine understanding of what this actually means may be compromised, leading to "measures" that are really not very good. Even obtaining a score on some measure often considered the gold standard in a particular area (e.g., the Beck Depression Inventory for depressed clients) is of little usefulness if the client does not truly comprehend the questions being asked or the instructions they have been given. And some social work clients are illiterate. A careful appraisal of the client's reading, writing, and language skills is required before simply inviting a person to participate in some approach to measurement.

An even subtler problem is the client whose cultural norms may be different than those from which an assessment instrument was originally developed. Apparently straightforward terms used in an RAI or IFS may have quite disparate meanings for people from differing cultures. In some cases, good translations of RAIs from English to other languages are available and may be used, but, even within different cultures and ethnicities, great variation can occur. Native speakers of Spanish may have been raised in Spain, Argentina, or the southwestern United States, and what appears to be their common first language is no guarantee that they will respond similarly to a Spanish translation of an RAI. Think of the not-so-subtle differences in how English speakers from Scotland, South Africa, Australia, or New York City use the same language to gain a sense of the differences among people whose first language may be Spanish or Chinese.

These issues, while present and relevant, are not unique to the arena of practice evaluation—they also often occur in everyday social work practice and must also be taken into account and dealt with in some manner. This requires experience, a keen awareness of the issue of how bias can creep into one's assessment methods (whether used for clinical or evaluation purposes), and taking proactive steps to ascertain whether the client genuinely understands what is being asked. The forms of assessment perhaps least subjective relate to recording observable behavior. But, even here, problems may emerge. Clients asked to self-record their own behaviors and to provide this information to the social worker may under- or over-report their activities to please the clinicians, to avoid embarrassment, to look good, and so forth. Individuals in the client's life who are recruited to record the client's actions may have an ax to grind or have other motivations to distort the client's records. An angry spouse keeping track of a client's use of alcohol or other drugs may over-report alcohol use or a benign parent keeping track of an abusive partner's interactions with their children may under-report child abuse for fear of having the children removed from the home. But, again, these are serious issues in assessment that apply to both practice and evaluation activities, and most social workers are aware of the potential for bias to occur and try to effectively deal with this.

3

Single-System Designs

GENERAL PRINCIPLES AND NOTATION

Are you ready for your first quiz? Here goes:

Who made the following three statements?

1. "Every treatment is an experiment."

2. "Special efforts should be made to ascertain whether abnormal manifestations are *increasing* or *decreasing* in number and intensity, as this often has a practical bearing on the management of the case."

3. "In work with individuals, averages mean very little."

Here are your choices:

A. Walter Hudson

B. Mary Richmond

C. Harry Hopkins

D. Allen Rubin

E. Eileen Gambrill

You might be surprised to learn that all three assertions came from Mary Richmond's influential textbook, *Social Diagnosis*, originally published in 1917. As you shall see in this chapter, single-system designs are an excellent way to operationalize these very early views by this extremely influential social work pioneer.

The approach toward the evaluation of social work practice known as single-system designs (SSDs) has been around for several decades. The earliest known publication using this approach in social work was authored by social worker Bill Butterfield and psychologist Arthur Staats and appeared in 1965 describing an intervention designed to enhance the reading skills of a Hispanic adolescent. Social worker Richard Stuart (1967) used these designs in his evaluation of a weight-control program two years later, and, by the early 1970s, a large number of illustrative and methodological articles, chapters, and books had appeared on the topic. A bibliography on single-system designs used in social work, covering the years 1965–1990, found over 250 citations (Thyer & Thyer, 1992), and the field has grown appreciably since then. What, exactly, are SSDs? Well, the *Social Work Dictionary* (Barker, 2003) provides the following definition:

> **Single-subject design.** A research procedure often used in clinical situations to evaluate the effectiveness of an intervention. The behavior of a single subject, such as an individual client, is used as a comparison and a control. Typically the results of progress or change are plotted graphically. Single-subject design is also known as $N=1$ (with N meaning number of persons) design or single-system design. (p. 399)

Rubin and Babbie (2005) define it as follows:

> **Single-case evaluation design.** A time-series design used to evaluate the impact of an intervention or a policy change on individual cases or systems.

For the balance of this book, we will use the abbreviation SSD to refer to single-system research designs. The term "single-*system* design" is preferred because these designs are not limited to investigations with single individuals. Rather, they can be applied to virtually any type of client system amenable to being repeatedly assessed over time. This can include a single person or a couple, a family, a small group, an organization, a city, county, state, or even a country—hence the term system rather than subject, which implies only an individual level of analysis. The research phobic will be glad to learn that basic SSDs have only two prerequisites:

1. That some reliable and valid outcome measure that assesses client–system functioning be available

2. That this outcome measure is actually repeatedly assessed over time

That is it. Nothing else is required. If this is done, however, the social worker is in a very good position to evaluate whether the client–system has *changed over time.* Or another way of putting it is to see if the client has gotten better, gotten worse, or has not changed. What SSDs do is to enable the practitioner to buttress his or her clinical judgment with corroborative empirical data that can be *convincing to others.* It is this quality of *public verifiability* that has the potential to elevate what the social worker does from the level of an art form or a purely subjective discipline to the realm of a scientifically credible profession. And it does not matter what the unit of analysis is, be it evaluating outcomes with a single person or at some higher level (e.g., statewide data): the design and logic of SSDs remain the same.

Moreover, if the social worker has some possibility of systematically introducing or removing the intervention, then sufficiently sophisticated SSDs that have the potential to permit genuine causal inferences regarding the effects of treatment become possible. Recall that evaluation research has two fundamental issues to address:

1. Did my client (or larger system) change?

2. If there were changes, how confident can I be that social work intervention caused those changes?

The first question can be called the evaluative question and the second the causal question. Both are immensely important to our field and to individual practitioners, but it is important to keep them separate and distinct, depending on the purposes of your evaluation efforts. Relatively simple SSDs can be used to answer the evaluative question, but more complex (and difficult to undertake) SSDs are needed to answer the causal question. Sometimes folks criticize an SSD because it did not do a good job of proving that social work treatment caused any observed improvements, but that is an unfair standard to apply if the intent of the study from the outset was to provide an answer only to the evaluative question.

SSDs can be arranged in a hierarchy of complexity ranging from the very simple to the very complex. We will review these designs in roughly this order and provide you with some real-life examples to flesh out the abstract concepts and to illustrate the practicality of these designs in various practice settings.

PREEXPERIMENTAL DESIGNS

The SSDs useful in simply determining if changes occurred (e.g., my client got better) can be called preexperimental because they usually do not permit you to make any causal inferences about the sources of those changes (e.g., my social work intervention caused the client to get better). Take a social worker in practice with an individual client who has a particular problem. As a part of assessment, the social worker located a reliable and valid, inexpensive, and culturally appropriate outcome measure that is a good means of measuring the client's problem or situation. Note: although we will most often refer to the client's "problem" in this chapter, it is important to recognize that one can equally use these designs to measure strengths, resources, or other, more positive, aspects of the client's life. At the same time the social worker begins treatment, she or he concurrently begins the regular assessment of the client, using the chosen outcome measure (it goes without saying that the use of these outcome measures should be acceptable to the client). If, over time, the outcome measure indicates positive changes, and these results corroborate the social worker's own clinical impressions and the client's informal reports, then the social worker has completed the rudiments of an SSD. The one remaining step is to prepare a simple line graph of the data for the client's file, a record that can be shared with the client, one's supervisor, or, in certain circumstances, other professionals.

The value of this type of study has been praised by Hawkins and Mathews (1999), who labeled it as Level-1 research, "systematically monitoring clinical outcomes—one's effects on client behavior—without any need to scientifically prove what is causing those effects" (p. 117). We believe that small-scale studies of this nature, with low internal validity, are to be encouraged as they promote the greater integration of social workers into the assessment of outcomes and build toward a more empirically based profession.

Here is a real example of using this approach. Social work intern Pam Birsinger was assigned to work with a client who suffered from moderate agoraphobia, a condition associated with marked anxiety in circumstances outside the home. Pam consulted some of the available empirical research on the treatment of agoraphobia (e.g., Thyer, 1987, and other resources) and asked the client, Mrs. Dorsett, to complete an RAI that measured the anxiety associated with agoraphobia, the CAS (see Westhuis & Thyer, 1989). Mrs. Dorsett did so a couple of times before Pam began an intervention called exposure therapy (ET). At that time (during the late 1980s) and still today, ET is one of the best supported psychosocial treatments for people with agoraphobia.

One of the situations Mrs. Dorsett had the most difficulty encountering was with a particularly large department store. As a part of treatment (and by no means the whole story), Pam accompanied Mrs. Dorsett to this store and, using support, encouragement, distraction, and reinforcement, along with some prior psychoeducational information she provided about the rationale for this approach, Pam asked the client to remain in the store until she became comfortable. This was in stark contrast to Mrs. Dorsett's usual practice of leaving as soon as she became frightened. Pam remained with Mrs. Dorsett and kept track of how long it took the client to indicate that she was calm. Thus, Pam's outcome measure for these (ET) sessions with Mrs. Dorsett was the *length of time* (in minutes) it took for the client to calm down. Obviously, if the ET sessions were helpful, it should take Mrs. Dorsett shorter periods of time to relax. Or, if ET was injurious, then she might never relax or might take longer and longer to do so rather than less and less time.

The results of the nine sessions of ET provided by Pam to Mrs. Dorsett are displayed in Figure 3.1. As can be seen, during the first session of ET, it took the client almost an hour to calm down. The subsequent sessions saw a rapid reduction in the length of time, then a spike during the fifth session, followed by four sessions of taking almost no time at all. Clearly, Mrs. Dorsett was becoming less fearful in this formerly avoided phobic situation, and this quantitative information corroborated Pam's clinical impressions of how the client was doing. Now suppose you were Pam's supervisor and you asked her, "Pam, how is your treatment with Mrs. Dorsett going?" If Pam told you something like, "Pretty well, I think. She is overcoming her fear of being in the department store that initially proved so troubling for her to remain in." You might be satisfied with this. But, if Pam showed you this graph with supplemental information to back up her assertion that Mrs. Dorsett was doing better at remaining in the department store, you would probably find it useful to corroborate her judgment (see Thyer & Birsinger, 1994).

Figure 3.1

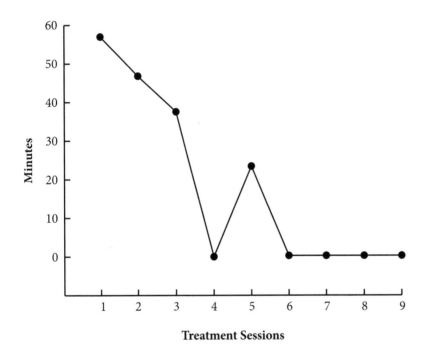

Treatment Sessions

This approach, taking measurements during treatment, can be called a *B design* in the vocabulary of SSDs, and it is about the simplest SSD there is. Can Pam claim that the data in Figure 3.1 *proves* that ET was helping Mrs. Dorsett? No, not at all. But can she claim to have some credible evidence that Mrs. Dorsett had gotten better over these nine sessions of ET? Sure. Note the element of plausibility here. We have no other information on Mrs. Dorsett. If, during these nine sessions of ET, she became suicidally depressed, psychotic, or addicted to crack, these data would not capture this at all. This is why the contention is made that SSD information can best be used to supplement the social worker's clinical judgments and impressionist views of changes in client functioning over time and not to replace such professional opinions. But when there is close congruence between clinical judgment and SSD data, the evidence is simply more convincing that something (hopefully positive) has transpired, and this is a good thing.

Here is another example of a social worker using a B design. Betsy Vonk, licensed clinical social worker (LCSW), was employed at the Emory University Student Counseling Center and received a referral for a new client, a 25-year-old graduate student named Beth. Beth's presenting problem was a severe fear of vaginal intercourse, secondary to a more generalized fear of vaginal penetration. She could not use tampons, tolerate a gynecological examination, have a Pap smear, or use a douche. She had been in therapy of an insight-oriented nature several times without any symptomatic improvement. Beth had a boyfriend and engaged in nonvaginal sex, but she sought help from Betsy to overcome her fears of vaginal penetration. Leaving out much of the clinical details here, Betsy conceptualized Beth's difficulty as a specific phobia, and the available evidence then (as now) suggested that one empirically supported treatment for specific phobias consists of (guess now), yes, our old friend, ET.

Betsy asked Beth to recruit Beth's boyfriend to assist her in overcoming this difficulty (something he readily agreed to do), and Betsy provided some psychoeducation with Beth about the nature and etiology of specific phobias and how they can usually be substantially overcome via ET. Under Betsy's guidance, Beth agreed to undertake a series of self-conducted homework exercises consisting of engaging in a mildly fear-evoking activity and persisting in it until she became calm. Betsy taught Beth to self-rate her anxiety on a zero-to-ten scale, with zero meaning she felt no anxiety and ten meaning she was panic-stricken. Beth was to report the maximum level of anxiety she experienced during her weekly "homework" and to see Betsy in between these exercises to discuss how things went and to plan future homework. Initially, Beth's homework consisted of her slightly inserting the tip of her own finger into her vagina and leaving it there for a minimum of 10 minutes. She was to do this at least three times that first week. This was repeated for the next two weeks (twice the first week and once the second). During weeks four and five, corresponding to counseling sessions four and five with Betsy, Beth agreed to more intense self-ET, including placing her finger deeper into her vagina and moving it. During the second session of this exercise, she found herself becoming sexually aroused, which initially frightened her, but not to a troubling degree. The sixth week, she invited her boyfriend to participate, and this went remarkably well, with her anxiety reducing to zero during the third practice session. During weeks seven and eight she had no homework exercises as her boyfriend was out of town, and she had exploratory counseling with the social worker. The ninth week, she and her boyfriend got so carried away that they spontaneously had vaginal intercourse, which was not only well tolerated by Beth, but was pleasurable and evoked little anxiety. Vaginal intercourse the following three weeks was also successful and free from anxiety. She later broke off the relationship with her boyfriend and entered a relationship with a new man. Sexual intercourse involving vaginal penetration continued to be experienced by the client as pleasurable, free from clinical anxiety.

These data are depicted in Figure 3.2 and also conform to the features of a B single-system research design. The primary outcome measure is the client's self-reported anxiety, with anecdotal supplemental reports of her successful sexual experiences. The treatment was ET over a 12-week period, which proved to seemingly result in the resolution of an intractable problem of a decade's duration (but, of course, we cannot be sure of this causal link). As a part of the social work counseling, Betsy provided information to Beth about safe sex and the importance of reliable condom use. This was a most interesting clinical presentation and outcome, and more information about the case can be found in Vonk and Thyer (1995) and Thyer and Vonk (2007). We'd like to stress that this was a very serious problem for Beth, and that the fairly rapid resolution of the problem should not be viewed as an indicator of its triviality to this client

The next most sophisticated type of SSD is called an *AB design*. As with the B design, systematic measures are taken of the client's situation during treatment, but this is preceded by the social worker getting some measures before treatment begins. This period is called a baseline, and, in the nomenclature of SSDs, is also labeled as an A phase. Thus, an AB design refers to taking some measures before treatment begins and then during treatment.

MSW student Krista Barker was interning at a vocational center serving individuals with developmental disabilities. One of her clients was John, a 23-year-old man with moderate mental retardation and a seizure disorder. A serious problem for John and the staff at the vocational center was his frequent display of inappropriate behavior including aggression such as taunting peers, engaging in verbal arguments, throwing objects, making threats of violence, noncompliance, leaving his work station;

Figure 3.2

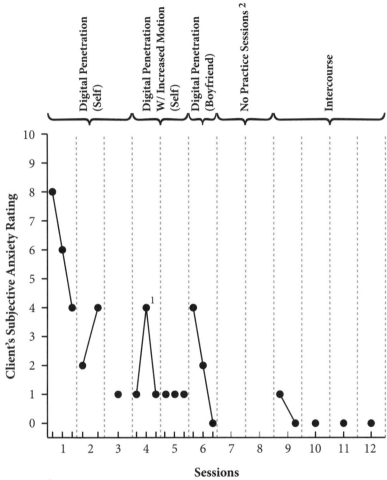

Sessions

[1] At this point, the client became aware of arosal. Subsequent sessions included arousal.

[2] The client's boyfriend was out of town. Client focused on ambivalence about her relationship.

physical aggression against staff and coworkers; verbal outbursts; and inappropriate sexual advances toward peers. These daily behaviors threatened the continuation of John's placement at the vocational center, and he was referred to Krista to try to help him reduce these inappropriate actions. Again, glossing over many of the clinical details here, Krista collected baseline information on John's problematic behavior over a five-day period and then implemented a reinforcement program wherein John would earn points for going for periods of time without displaying inappropriate behavior. Points could in turn be redeemed for social privileges. The time period needed to earn points was gradually increased from 15 to 20, to 30, and then 45 minutes, depending on how well he responded.

The data were collected by Krista based upon her direct observation of John from 9:00 a.m. to 2:00 p.m. daily. After five days of baseline, the new point system was implemented. Note that no punitive or aversive contingencies were employed. These AB data are displayed in Figure 3.3 and demonstrate that John's inappropriate social behaviors dramatically declined during the seven treatment days following the five-day baseline and virtually disappeared. The intervention was low cost, did not cause any disruption at work for John, and only required about 15 minutes of Krista's attention per day to administer. A serious problem that threatened John's continued placement at the vocational center was positively resolved by this social work intern within a two-week period. More details can be found in Barker and Thyer (2000).

Figure 3.3

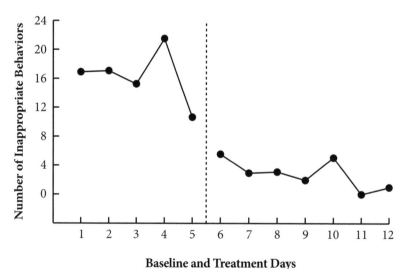

Baseline and Treatment Days
Total Number of Inappropriate Behaviors From 9:00 a.m.–2:00 p.m.

From a scientific perspective, a *prospectively* designed baseline possesses greater merits than a retrospectively designed one, but the latter type is certainly possible and sometimes appropriate. It may be that the clinical picture dictates that you not delay treatment for the purposes of gathering baseline data. In such cases, it may be possible to gather needed information retrospectively. This is most obviously possible when archival data of some sort are available. For example, one could evaluate a social policy by comparing social statistics on some variable for a few years prior to the establishment of a new law. School attendance or medical records may also be useful in this regard, as are diaries, personal planners, and so on.

But retrospectively created baselines based upon client recollections may be problematic. We, the authors, can barely recall what we had for lunch three days ago. Asking clients to recall information for retrospective baseline purposes may be a pretty unreliable method of gathering data except for very significant, but relatively infrequent events (for example, being abused, having a seizure, having sexual intercourse, etc.), not those happening many times per day.

In another example of an AB design, hospital social worker Lisa Baker was employed on a neonatal intensive care unit at a hospital in Atlanta. All of the babies cared for at the unit were medically fragile, and, when healthy enough to go home, the infants were often prescribed an infant apnea monitor, an electronic device secured around the baby's chest with a soft elastic strap that records each breath and heartbeat. Mothers would be instructed by nursing staff on the need for using the monitor each day and were trained in using it. Once home, the mothers were to be sure and use the monitor during most of the baby's sleeping time. If the baby stopped breathing or the heart slowed dangerously, the monitor would sound an alarm, often sufficient to startle the infant into a normal breathing pattern or heart rate and to summon Mom or another caregiver to resuscitate the child. The neonatal unit staff would call the mom weekly and ask that the monitor's data be electronically downloaded (over the phone) to the hospital, where the infant's status could be examined by a neonatalogist.

Lisa would get called in when, as frequently occurred, the caregivers did not reliably use the monitor, thus placing their baby at some risk. The nurses and pediatricians wanted the social worker to "fix" this problem and enhance the mothers' compliance with the prescribed monitor usage. Good empiricist that she is, Lisa consulted the research literature about this problem and found, to her dismay, that nothing had been published on the topic of promoting infant apnea monitor use by noncompliant parents. She then went to related literature on promoting adherence to other health care regimens, such as those for diabetics, people with high blood pressure, and other conditions requiring regular monitoring. From this information, she got some leads on developing an intervention that relied on home visits, frequent phone contact, education, making sure that the parents had access to a working phone, and reinforcement. One case she was involved with is depicted in Figure 3.4.

There are about 39 days of A-phase or baseline data depicting the hours of monitor use per day. This information was provided electronically from the monitor itself, which kept track of this variable. Lisa then worked with the mothers and obtained the data on monitor use over the next 32 days. While there is considerable variability in the data in the B phase, it is compellingly obvious that monitor use increased dramatically following Lisa's intervention compared to the baseline data. Further details on this innovative project, involving nine such cases, can be found in Baker and Thyer (1999, 2000).

The strength of SSDs lies in their flexibility. They are undertaken by social workers themselves, not by some outside evaluator who descends upon an agency and informs practitioners of what they need to be doing to help the evaluator. SSDs can be responsive with changes in clinical circumstances and can cost very little in terms of money or resources. And their intrusiveness in the clinical situation can be minimal. This flexibility is illustrated in the next case.

Do you recall Mrs. Dorsett, who experienced agoraphobia and was treated by Pam Birsinger? During the 10 weeks or so that Mrs. Dorsett was in treatment with Pam, she completed the CAS on a weekly basis, twice while Pam was providing her with some psychoeducational intervention about the nature and treatment of agoraphobia, but before formal ET began, and four times over the remaining seven weeks, during which time Pam provided ET. Now you will recall that a baseline period refers to a time when no formal treatment is being provided, but, certainly, a phase during which a psychoeducational intervention is being provided is not the same as no treatment at all. In this case, we can call the phase of psychoeducation treatment a B phase, and the phase when a different treatment was provided (ET) a C phase. This could be called a BC single-system research design, wherein the client is sequentially provided

Figure 3.4

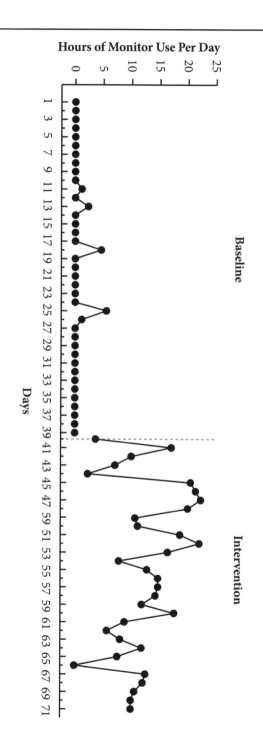

two different active treatments (labeled B and C) that are compared, as opposed to an AB design that compares client functioning during active treatment relative to the client's functioning during a no treatment or baseline condition.

The data with respect to Mrs. Dorsett in this circumstance are displayed in Figure 3.5. She completed the CAS twice and each time scored in the "clinical range," which is typically displayed by persons with agoraphobia (usually around 30 points or higher, but you'd need some familiarity with the CAS and its background research to know this). Her CAS scores seemed to drop a bit during the C phase (when ET was provided), compared to the B phase when Pam delivered only psychoeducational intervention, and her scores remained below the clinical cutting score associated with the CAS, which is good. Again, imagine you are Pam's supervisor and you ask, "How is Mrs. Dorsett doing?" If Pam says she is doing fine and provides you with the graph in Figure 3.5, you would likely have some enhanced confidence that your supervisee was competently caring for this one client.

Figure 3.5

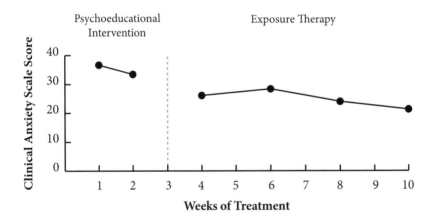

EXPERIMENTAL DESIGNS

Now so far we have discussed SSDs solely as a means of assessing outcomes and gathering credible information to support one's clinical impressions that a client is getting better or not. How might it be possible using this SSD approach to draw conclusions that a given treatment caused some observed changes? In order to do this, it must be possible to manipulate the introduction or removal of a social work intervention in some manner or to use baselines of varying lengths. In some situations, when these conditions can be arranged, causal inference at the level of the individual case (or system) may be possible.

You will recall that, in an AB design, we can examine client functioning in the absence of treatment, before it begins in other words. This is a very good example of that hoary social work dictum of *beginning where the client is at*. Assessing the client's functioning or state of being before treatment begins is useful. Using reliable and valid measures is even more so. Doing this several times is better yet. This is why Mary Richmond (1917) made the statement cited at the beginning of this chapter:

> Special efforts should be made to ascertain whether abnormal manifestations are increasing or decreasing in number and intensity, as this often has a practical bearing on the management of the case. (p. 435)

Now imagine an AB design where the data during the baseline are clearly stable. And it is found, during the subsequent B phase, that the data appear to continue on unchanged from the baseline. They neither change their level nor direction nor slope. Would you be tempted to say that treatment caused any changes? No. In fact, you might even be willing to assert that treatment had no effect on your outcome measure. Now suppose the opposite. The baseline data in an AB design are clearly stable, then the B phase begins, and the data are immediately observed to dramatically improve to an amazing extent. Suppose further that the baseline was very long indeed, and the client's problem is one generally known to be pretty severe and intractable—not very labile, subject to spontaneous remission, or amenable to placebo influences. Moreover, these improvements in the baseline condition continue on, very improved, and very stable for a very long period. Confess it, wouldn't you be tempted to claim that treatment B caused the improvements in client functioning? Wouldn't you like to be able to proudly claim, "Here is evidence that my social work treatment was effective in helping my client improve?" Let's face it, under such circumstances, anyone would be tempted to make such a causal inference. Such unambiguous situations, however, remain rare. Changes are not usually so clear-cut, durable, or impactful on an intractable problem.

Simply inferring changes in data obtained from a single client (or system) is usually done by an examination of how the data differ between phases, such as between an A phase and a B phase, and looking at features such as *level, slope,* and *variability*. If there are no obvious shifts in the data on these dimensions, then one may usually infer that no meaningful effects occurred. This is a relatively easy judgment to make, so long as one applies the following conservative test:

> *If changes between phases are not visually clear and obvious, then they do not exist!*

Through application of this standard, you will be very unlikely to assert that a change occurred when it really did not. You might, however, miss some small treatment effects that, although not visually obvious, are nonetheless real. In scientific research, this is called making a *Type II error*, asserting that there are no differences when there really are some. The opposite, claiming that there are differences, when there really are not any, is called a *Type I error*. Within the tradition of SSD research, making a Type II error means that, yes some treatments that exert small effects may be overlooked, but this is seen as a useful filter in that we usually are not interested in treatments that produce *small* effects. We want interventions that produce *big* effects—striking, positive improvements.

You can look at changes in the overall level of the data. If the baseline closely fluctuates around, say, the 20% level of some outcome measure, and then, immediately after the application of the intervention, the data in the B phase jump up to and remain hovering around the 80% level, you are more likely to think that a real change occurred. But, if the change was from around 20% to around 23%, you might either miss it by simply looking at the data or not be very impressed with the impact of B, even if you did pick up on this amount of change.

You can also look at changes in the slope of the data. If the A-phase data are tending upward at, say, a 10-degree angle, then, during the B phase, the slope immediately changes to, say, 60 degrees and stays there, you are more likely to conclude that B had an effect than if the change in slope was from 10 to 15 degrees.

And sometimes you can look at changes in the variability of the data in each phase, useful in assessing the clinical status and response to treatment for otherwise highly labile problems. Say the A-phase data on the mood of someone who meets the

DSM criteria for rapid-cycling bipolar disorder reflect great shifts up and down for some period of time, then, immediately after treatment B is introduced, the mood shifts diminish considerably and remain much more stable for another reasonable period of time. Again, you'd be more likely to infer a positive effect of intervention B than if the variability in the data remained very high.

So one way you can make inferences about change in SSDs is to look at changes in these three dimensions of the data between phases and at changes in level, slope, and variability. But, even in the best of cases, with a B or AB design, you can't really be certain that intervention B caused any improvements because of the wide array of possible other influences that may have had an impact on your client, influences collectively known *as threats to internal validity*. Changes unknown to you in the client's diet, medication, living circumstances, interpersonal relationships, illness or recovery, illegal substance abuse, or big events in the media (e.g., a terrorist attack) can all affect your client or system, and, if these changes occur around the time you introduce intervention B, causal inference may be compromised.

How can we get around this problem? One of the best ways is by replicating an effect. What is meant by replication? Here are a few definitions:

> Generally the duplication of a study to expose or reduce error or the reintroduction or removal of an intervention to increase the internal validity of a quasiexperiment or single-case design evaluation. (Rubin & Babbie, 2005, p. 755)

The logic goes as follows: "A treatment effect is suggested if the dependent variable responds similarly each time the treatment is introduced and removed, with the direction of responses being different for the introductions compared with the removals" (Shadish, Cook, & Campbell, 2002, p. 190). For example, suppose you have an AB design, and, with the introduction of B, a large, positive effect is noted. This is good. If you should happen then to stop providing intervention B (in other words, return to the baseline condition of no treatment), and the outcome measure promptly deteriorates, you have not one, but two examples of an effect of treatment B: one (positive) when it was applied and a second (deterioration) when it was removed. With two such apparent demonstrations of an effect on the client coincident with the introduction or removal of social work intervention, it is harder for the skeptic to argue that something else had transpired in the client's life, something that just coincidentally happened to occur around the same time as your treatment was applied and then removed. Now, if you should reintroduce B and find another marked improvement, you have three successive demonstrations of an effect of B: two showing that when B is applied the problem gets better and one showing that when B is removed the problem gets worse. For most skeptics, this would be pretty convincing evidence of a causal link (or, perhaps more solidly stated philosophically, a functional relationship) existing between B and changes in the client's functioning.

The above hypothetical description is of an ABAB design, a baseline condition followed by a treatment phase, a second baseline phase, and succeeded by a second treatment phase. Within the language of SSDs, this approach and its variations are called withdrawal designs because the treatment is withdrawn. Sometimes this withdrawal can be deliberate for the purposes of demonstrating the intervention's effectiveness to the client, social worker, or both. Of course, the deliberate introduction of a withdrawal phase should only be undertaken if the issues at hand are not seriously harmful or life threatening and only with the client's (or guardian's) consent. Or they can occur naturally as a part of the termination process of social work treatment, which is certainly a legitimate justification in many circumstances. And sometimes withdrawals can be unplanned or accidental, as occurred in a report by Miller and Miller (1970).

A social worker was helping organize a community self-help group for individuals receiving welfare payments. During the initial three meetings, attendance dropped from seven to four to zero people. This was graphed as the data in an A phase of an SSD. The social worker then introduced a system of providing reinforcers in return for attending meetings, an array of goods (toys, clothing, and appliances), services (day camp scholarships, help in negotiating with police, and help in finding a house), and information (birth control), all of which were donated to the social worker for this purpose. During the next eight meetings, attendance ranged from eight to 21 people, with an average of 15. These data formed the B phase. Things were looking really good in terms of attendance when disaster struck. The social worker had to be admitted to the hospital for unscheduled surgery and was absent for the next eight meetings. Attendance ranged from zero to 11, with no one attending five of the eight meetings. This constituted the second A phase.

When the social worker was back on her feet, she resumed the reinforcement program, and attendance immediately popped up from zero (the last three meetings of the second A phase) to 22, ranging from eight to 22, with an average of around 15. This constituted the second B phase of this ABAB study. There clearly appeared to be a causal relationship between the social worker's intervention and attendance at this self-help group for welfare recipients. There was also good evidence that attendance at these meetings generalized to other self-help areas of the clients' lives, with an increase in participation in other civic groups wherein attendance was not artificially rewarded. This simple study is a nice example of using an unanticipated withdrawal of services and their reintroduction to create an ABAB design, and it provides useful leads for social workers seeking to promote attendance at meetings among clients receiving welfare.

The experimental logic here can be called the *Principle of Unlikely Successive Coincidences*. One significant shift in the data in, say, an AB SSD, can perhaps be explained by chance. But *three* such shifts is highly unlikely to be because of some coincidental influences that just happened to occur when the social worker applied or removed a treatment.

Here is another example of using an ABAB design to try to demonstrate that an intervention is responsible for changes in clients. One of the authors (Thyer) was a consultant at a group home for individuals with a history of long-term institutionalization for chronic mental illness. The home's activity director was having problems in coming up with an exercise program that the residents would participate in. She had found it very hard, for example, to induce the heavily medicated residents to get up at 7:00 a.m. with her to watch and participate in an aerobics program on television at that time. She consulted the social worker to see if something could be worked out.

A used stationary exercise bike was acquired and set up in the living room in a place where the TV would be easily seen. A notebook was kept nearby, and the residents were told that they could use the bike to exercise anytime they wanted, but to please notify the staff when they were going to do so, so that mileage from the bike's odometer could be recorded. Data were recorded for one week (the first A phase) and, sadly, the bike was very rarely used. At this point, the social worker arranged for the activity therapist to provide the residents with small reinforcers (consumables), contingent upon riding the bike. Data were collected over the next week (the first B phase), and bike riding was found to have considerably increased. While this looked great, and the activity therapist was very pleased, we knew that it may have been a fluke, that maybe something else could have happened to enhance bike riding around the same time the reinforcement program was implemented. So, given that this was not a life-threatening or urgent circumstance, we discontinued the reinforcement program while still making the bike freely accessible to the residents. Bike riding plummeted. So now we have two apparent demonstrations of experimental control over riding an exercise bike: an increase when the intervention was applied (the first B phase) and a decrease when it was discontinued (the second A phase). While this was interesting, we were left with sedentary residents. Thus, the program was reinstated

Figure 3.6

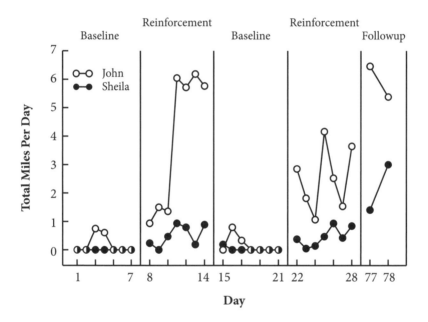

(the second B phase), and the results examined to again reveal marked increases in bike riding. Wonderful! The activity therapist decided to leave the low-cost reinforcement in place as a permanent part of the group home's programming. Two months later, we checked on the amount of riding that occurred on two days, and it remained quite high (see Figure 3.6).

With this ABAB design, we have three demonstrations of the apparent effects of the intervention with nice data shifts evident between the first A and B phases, the first B and second A, and the second A and second B. Within the field of SSD ,this is considered to be quite compelling data that the intervention caused changes in riding the exercise bike. Further details can be found in Thyer, Irvine, and Santa (1984).

Here is another, completely different illustration of an ABAB design with sufficiently compelling data to make causal inferences plausible. Back in the 1980s, Florida did not require automobile drivers or passengers to buckle their safety-belts. Within the context of an evaluation research class, one of the authors (Thyer) undertook the following study. A supply of adhesive stickers reading "Safety-Belt Use Required in this Vehicle" was acquired from the state highway patrol. All students in the author's MSW class were asked to begin recording whether each passenger they drove in their own car buckled up spontaneously, to keep track of all such passengers on a daily basis, to record this on a data sheet that was provided by the instructor, and to bring this information to class. This was collected by the instructor weekly. Not all students had cars or drove passengers, and some students drove more passengers than others, but, nevertheless, for each day of the week, it was possible to aggregate the total number of people driven by the MSW students and whether they buckled up. The dependent variable in this study was the percentage of passengers who buckled up each day. Students were asked for the purposes of this class project to consistently use their own safety-belts when they drove a passenger (this controlled for modeling influences on the part of the driver).

After two weeks of data collection, constituting the first baseline or A phase, the students were given the dashboard stickers and asked to attach them to the right-front passenger's dashboard and to continue data collection as before. If asked about the sticker by a passenger, they were to reply in a pleasant tone, "Well, I always prefer that my passengers buckle up," but to not use any other threats or cajolery. Two more weeks of data collection followed (the first B phase). The baseline safety-belt use of passengers was about 35%, and, during the B phase, was over 70%, a clear doubling of safety-belt use. So far, so good, but still not a convincing effect from a strictly scientific point of view. Maybe there had been a horrible accident in town around the time the stickers were introduced, sensitizing everyone to the value of seat belts? To provide for a more robust analysis of the prompting stickers, the students were asked to remove them and to take data for a further two weeks. Safety-belt use dropped immediately to around 40%. Good for the purposes of experimental control, but clearly not a healthy state of affairs for the passengers, so a second B phase was introduced and fresh stickers applied by the students to their cars. Up popped safety-belt use to nearly 80% (see Figure 3.7). Again, we have three replications of an effect of the independent variable (intervention, in this case, dashboard stickers prompting safety-belt use): two showing increases when the intervention was applied and one showing the expected decrease when it was removed. Because causal inference is possible with certain SSDs, depending on the quality of the

Figure 3.7

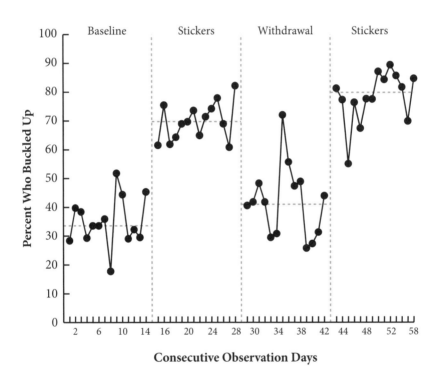

data observed, they can legitimately be described as *experimental designs*.

CAN SELECTED SSDs BE CONSIDERED ACTUAL EXPERIMENTS?

We have used the term experimental to describe selected types of SSDs that may possess high internal validity. You may question our use of this adjective, perhaps because you associate experiments only with the use of GRDs like those described in the next chapter. We take a broader perspective in describing what is meant by a genuine experiment, one that is consistent with many authorities in the area of research methodology. For example, Shadish, Cook, and Campbell (2002) provide several different definitions of experiments that support the view that SSDs may qualify as experiments:

> A test under controlled conditions that is made to demonstrate a known truth, examine the validity of a hypothesis, or *determine the efficacy of something previously untried* [italics added]. (p. 1)
>
> A study in which an intervention is deliberately introduced to observe its effects. (p. 12)
>
> One or more independent variables are manipulated to observe their effects on one or more dependent variables. (p. 12)

A similar perspective is expressed by Corsini (2002):

> **Experiment.** The manipulation of one or more independent variables conducted under controlled conditions to test one or more hypotheses, especially for making inferences of a cause-and-effect character. Involves the measurement of one or more dependent variables. (p. 351)

By these standards, the ABAB studies described above represent genuine experiments. This is worth stressing because sometimes our social work textbooks equate the term *experiment* with only one type of design: the randomized, controlled trial involving large numbers of people. This is clearly incorrect, given the definitions provided above. The defining characteristic of an experimental design is its ability to isolate cause-and-effect relationships between an intervention and an outcome, not the sample size or the existence of control groups. Appropriate controls are indeed needed in genuinely experimental research to account for various threats to internal validity. In nomothetic research, control *groups* of various types may well be needed to control for threats such as the passage of time, maturation, concurrent historical events, and so on. But, in SSDs, such control is achieved through different mechanisms, such as baselines and withdrawal phases. The purpose is the same—to control for rival explanations apart from the intervention that may influence the outcomes—but there are many ways this can be achieved apart from randomized controlled studies. Some fields make great use of experiments, yet the methodology of randomized controlled trials is largely absent from their scientific research projects in fields such as chemistry, physics, or engineering. A chemist seeking to learn the result of combining two chemicals does not try to obtain a random selection of the chemicals or use a control condition of placing two chemicals side by side in separate test tubes. The chemist obtains a typical sample of the chemicals, combines them, and observes the result. This is done a number of times, and, if similar results follow, the chemist becomes pretty sure she or he knows what will happen. If other chemists worldwide replicate her or his findings independently, then the results become more conclusively established as a generalizable fact.

A less robust, but nevertheless often convincing design is the ABA design, which provides only two possible demonstrations of an effect of treatment, but is still a considerable improvement over the AB design in terms of its internal validity. An example is provided by Thyer, Thyer, and Massa (1991). A senior citizens' center in Tallahassee offered a free lunch, and a large number of people came to the center to enjoy this meal, many driving their own cars and parking in the center's lot. At the time of this project, Florida did not have a mandatory safety-belt use law, and most of the seniors driving from the center's lot after lunch were informally observed to have not been wearing their over-the-shoulder safety-belt. We undertook the following study as a class project, associated again with an MSW evaluation research course.

Two observers stood across the street from the parking lot's exit and unobtrusively recorded the safety-belt use of each driver as he or she exited the lot after lunch. The two observers (MSW students) recorded this information independently of each other, and a reliability check showed that they agreed on average about 84% of the time, indicating that our outcome measure (percentage of drivers buckled up each day) was a reliable one. After seven days of baselining safety-belt use, we introduced our intervention: a female MSW student who stood at the lot's exit holding a colored placard reading "Please Buckle Up. I Care" on one side (initially displayed to exiting drivers) and the phrase "Thanks for Buckling Up!" on side two, displayed if the driver was seen buckling up after reading the sign or was already buckled. This was a friendly, noncoercive approach to reminding seniors to use their safety-belts. Data collection continued as before during this B phase for 14 days and for an additional six days of a return to baseline condition. The results are depicted in Figure 3.8. During the first baseline, safety-belt use was clearly not increasing or decreasing, and an average of about 42% of exiting drivers buckled with no prompting. During the B phase, safety-belt use quickly increased and averaged

60% over the two weeks, dropping to about 48% during the second B phase. While not as compelling as the data presented in the earlier ABAB studies we described, Figure 3.8 makes a pretty plausible case that displaying the prompting signs was effective at producing a modest increase in the safety-belt use of these drivers. Logistics prevented us from continuing this program indefinitely, but it was a valuable learning experience for the MSW students in that we could graph our data each week and see patterns emerge. In this study, as in the dashboard sticker study, students' grades were not related to how the data turned out or whether the intervention proved successful. However, drawing from the results of this study, another social work student, Melvin Williams, completed his doctoral dissertation by evaluating the effects of regularly formatted metal traffic signs mounted at parking lot exits reading "Fasten Safety-belt." Melvin, too, used SSDs to evaluate the effects of these signs, which did prove modestly effective in promoting safety-belt use (see Williams, Thyer, Bailey, & Harrison, 1989). Regularly mounted metal traffic signs at parking lot exits are a much more practical approach to enhancing safety-belt use than placards displayed by MSW students, but doing the latter study set the stage for the development of Melvin's project.

It is worth noting that designs whose internal validity is dependant on using withdrawal designs like the ABA and the ABAB must involve interventions whose effects can be expected to be temporary and that the outcome measure will deteriorate once the intervention is removed. This limitation is very common (perhaps unfortunately so) among social work interventions, but would not be present with

Figure 3.8

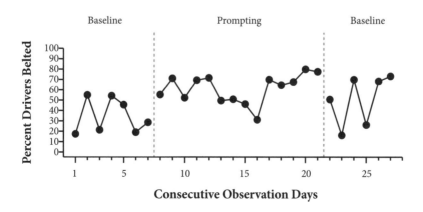

treatments that produce some sort of enduring or even permanent change. Examples might include counseling methods aimed at helping the client develop insight into his or her situation. If such counseling were being provided and such insights occurred, enabling the client to better cope with his or her situation, simply discontinuing the counseling in the context of an ABAB design does not mean that magically all of the insight and self-awareness the client developed will evaporate. If intervention helped the client acquire some sort of skill, say, a social skill, like becoming a better job interviewee or being able to solve math problems or if it resulted in the alleviation of an anxiety disorder, again, halting treatment should not automatically produce an immediate relapse. Yet, if the data do not regress to some extent when treatment is discontinued, the experimental logic of the ABA and ABAB collapses, and you end up with, in effect, data looking as if they came from simply an AB design. This is fine from a clinical standpoint, in that following a baseline, the client got better, and, when treatment was discontinued (as in an ABA design), she or he retained his or her gains and did not relapse. And most social workers would be very pleased with such a result. But, on those rare occasions when you have a real need to demonstrate that treatment caused client improvements, these designs relying on withdrawal phases to help demonstrate experimental control may not be useful. What else can you do?

Another form of experimental SSD is called the *multiple-baseline design* (MBLs). There are three types of MBLs:

1. MBL Design Across Subjects

This is used when you have two or more clients with the same problem who will receive the same treatment, and you wish to demonstrate not only that the client got better, but that your intervention is responsible for these improvements.

2. MBL Design Across Problems

This is used when you have one client with two or more problems, each of which will be sequentially treated with the same intervention, and you wish to demonstrate that your intervention caused improvements in these problems.

3. MBL Design Across Settings

This is used when you have one client with the same problem occurring in two or more settings, and you plan to treat the problems sequentially in the different settings using the same intervention. This would also be used to demonstrate that your treatment program was responsible for any improvements in the problem in these different settings.

Let us look at each of these designs individually.

Doctoral student Karen Sowers was looking for a dissertation topic. Her own child, Michael, was attending a church-affiliated school, and many of the children were driven to the school by their parents in the morning and picked up in the afternoon. Karen had some personal reasons to be concerned about the nonuse of seat belts by elementary school kids and got the school to agree to allow her to develop an intervention to promote safety-belt use by the children and to evaluate it. First Karen arranged for independent observers to monitor safety-belt use as kids were picked up at the end of the school day. These were children for whom over-the-shoulder safety-belts were appropriate, they were not small enough for car seats. At the time, Florida did not have any laws mandating child safety-belt use. By observing over 100 of the kids over a number of days, Karen identified 16 who were observed to *never* use their seat belts. These were the children she focused her data collection on when she applied her intervention to all the school children.

Karen consulted relevant empirical literature and came up with an interventive package involving education, modeling, manual practice, assertiveness training for the children aimed at the parents (e.g., "Daddy, Daddy, don't go, I am not buckled up!" or "Thanks, Mommy, for helping me buckle up. That means you love me!"), and reinforcement. She divided her 16 nonusers into two groups of eight; one would get the intervention first, and the second group of eight would receive it sometime later. She baselined safety-belt use for both groups of eight kids, and her outcome measure was the percentage of children in each group who were observed to get buckled up as they were driven away from school in the afternoon. For example, if four of the eight were buckled on a given day, then the data point for that day would be 50%.

The results of this MBL across subjects (in this case, the unit of analysis was the repeated measurement of safety-belt use by each *group* of eight kids) are depicted in Figure 3.9. The children in the top group did not use their safety-belts at all during the eight days baseline. This can be considered a (*very*) stable baseline. The intervention was applied, and immediately all kids in Group 1 began buckling up. Their safety-belt use remained very high for over three weeks. At follow-up, months later, safety-belt use remained very high, even though the intervention had been completely discontinued at day 35. This top portion of the graph by itself could be considered an ABA design with no deterioration of effect and logically identical to an AB design with only *one* apparent change in the outcome measure, coincident with the introduction of treatment.

But look at the second group. Their baseline lasted about seven days longer, and a few kids began buckling up about the time the first group got their training. Nevertheless, the last three days of the second group's baseline showed a reduction in safety-belt use and trended in the opposite direction that Karen anticipated her intervention to produce, so she began the training program for these eight kids about day 15. Again, there was an immediate increase in safety-belt use lasting several weeks, and, at follow-up months later, belt use remained high. Again, looking at the bottom portion of the graph alone, it looks like an ABA design, with no regression during the second A phase, so this is logically like another AB design. However, by tracking two groups of kids concurrently and only seeing very large increases on the two occasions Karen started her training program, the experimental logic is stronger than if she had an AB design alone. She has two demonstrations of an apparent effect, not just one, thus enhancing the internal validity of her study, that is, the credibility of claiming that it was the intervention alone that produced these improvements.

Now you may be wondering about the small, temporary increases in safety-belt use at the end of the baseline of Group 2. So did Karen. When she inquired, it turned out that two siblings with different last names were assigned to different groups, and when, sibling 1 in Group 1 got trained, the second sibling in Group 2 was affected by her sibling's behavior. Fortunately, the effect was small and temporary, so the overall internal validity of Karen's conclusion ("My training program *caused* these kids to buckle up.") was not seriously compromised. Some months later, Karen was contacted by the chief of the Florida Head Start Program who requested a copy of her safety-belt training curriculum to implement it statewide. Now that is a great outcome, illustrating how practice-research can influence policy on a large-scale basis (see Sowers-Hoag, Thyer, & Bailey, 1987).

MSW intern Nell Maeser used an MBL design across subjects on a smaller scale with three male adolescents who met the *DSM* criteria for severe mental retardation. Nell was interning at an intermediate care facility of the mentally retarded (ICFMR) and was asked to help the boys to acquire some proper table manners. When eating, the boys often would eat with their hands, squabble over food, spill, dribble, and, in general, display a less-than-pleasing aesthetic experience to observers. This inhibited staff efforts to prepare these young men for community integration. Nell reviewed some prior empirical social work literature on enhancing the eating practices and utensil use of people with various disabilities (e.g., Blackman, Gehle, & Pinkston, 1979; Butterfield & Parson, 1973), as well as some outcome studies found in other disciplines (e.g., Song & Ghandi, 1974; Wilson, Reid, Phillips, & Burgio, 1984) and came up with a provisional training protocol intended to help her three young clients properly serve themselves during family-style dining. The ICFMR staff had deemed this to be an important skill for these youths to acquire, especially because it inhibited the boys from community outings to dine in restaurants.

The basic skills involved serving oneself food (cereal, applesauce, scrambled eggs, etc.) from a large bowl to one's own bowl or plate using a large spoon. Nell broke down this task into nine sequential steps (e.g., (1) hold the serving bowl in both hands; (2) place the serving bowl within one inch of one's plate, etc.) and base-lined each child separately in terms of his ability to serve himself neatly from a large bowl. Nell served as the trainer, and observers recorded the number of steps correctly performed from the task sequence during each trial. As can be seen in Figure 3.9, during the baseline for the first child, Peter, no steps in the task sequence were correctly performed. After Nell began her teaching program, Peter gradually acquired this skill. Similar patterns were displayed for the other two kids, Danny and Michael. In that the skill was absent during the baseline and was subsequently acquired when Nell began her teaching program, there can be little doubt from these data that it was Nell's teaching program that helped these kids acquire this useful skill. Want details? Check out Maeser and Thyer (1990).

Figure 3.9

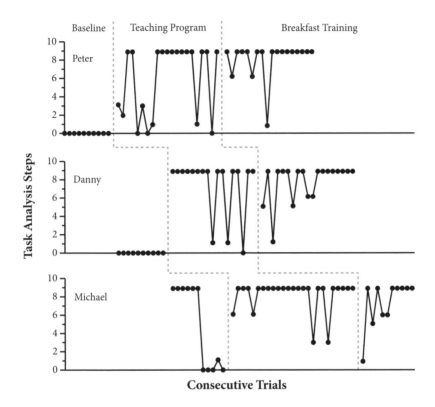

The above two examples involved using an MBL design across subjects design as a means of trying to establish a causal relationship between an intervention and an improvement in clients. Note that this involved using different clients with the same problem and receiving the same treatment. If they had had different problems or had received different treatments, then the internal validity of this type of MBL design would have been compromised because you would not have seen a replication of the same effect over the same set of conditions (same apparent effect resulting from the same intervention).

The logic of the other variations of the MBL designs is identical. In the MBL across problems, you have a client with different problems sequentially treated with the same intervention. As an example, say our client, let's call him Allen, suffers from specific phobias from three different things: spiders, snakes, and dogs.

We could baseline Allen's separate phobias, and then, with stable baseline data, apply a psychosocial intervention to *one* of Allen's phobias let's say spiders, using a treatment such as real-life gradual desensitization. While monitoring Allen's response to treatment for his spider phobia, we continue to baseline the severity of his (untreated) phobias to snakes and dogs. If his spider phobia improves, we could then apply the same intervention to another fear, say, snakes, while baselining his untreated phobia of dogs. If his snake phobia then improves while the dog phobia remains severe, we could then treat this remaining fear. If his dog phobia then improved, we would have had three successful replications of an apparent effect: gradual ET reduces specific phobias. If the initial baselines were stable, and the baselines of the untreated phobias reflected continuing severe fears even after the treated one(s) responded favorably, the social worker would have strongly plausible and logical grounds for concluding that this treatment caused these improvements in this client, thus qualifying this study's design and outcomes as an experimental investigation.

Now the logic of this design assumes that you have a highly specific intervention. A treatment aimed at producing generalized improvements across all areas of client functioning, such as, say, insight-oriented psychotherapy, a coping skill, or a tranquilizing medication, would not be amenable to experimental analysis in this manner since all three phobias could plausibly be improved as soon as treatment began for the first one.

The third type of MBL design to be discussed is the MBL across settings design. It requires that you have one client (or system) that has the same problem occurring in different contexts to be treated with the same approach. The purpose is to "prove" that the treatment "caused" improvements in this problem occurring in these differing settings. Suppose the client is an individual who meets the *DSM* criteria for schizophrenia, and, although the client's functioning is fairly stable on a particular medication regimen, he or she continues to have bizarre verbal outbursts in the group home where he or she lives, in the vocational program where he or she works, and during evening general equivalency diploma (GED) classes. You are able to get staff and teachers to reliably record the frequency of these verbal outbursts, and they are baselined across these three settings. The intervention is a low-cost reinforcement program, wherein the client is informed (and this is actually carried out) that, by refraining from bizarre outbursts, he or she can earn points, chips, or tokens, redeemable periodically for desired items or consumables. Initially, the duration is set low and is readily attainable, and it is then lengthened (and perhaps the reinforcers enhanced) as the client is successful in reducing outbursts. This intervention could be applied in one setting, say the group home, and its effects monitored, while outbursts continued to be baselined in the other two settings. If it were apparently success-ful in the group home, it could next be applied during the vocational program, while continuing to baseline outbursts during evening GED classes. If appar-ently successful in this second setting, it could then be applied in the remaining one. If you found that the baselined outbursts in all three settings were stable and then reduced following intervention in one initial setting, but not the other two and then found reductions only when the same intervention was sequen-tially applied in the remaining settings, you would have strong, logical grounds for concluding that your program caused the observed reductions in bizarre outbursts. If your inner philosopher of science makes you uncomfortable with the language of causation, call it *demonstrating a functional relationship between a treatment and an outcome,* if you find that more palatable.

HOW TO REPORT AND INTERPRET DATA

There are various schools of thought with respect to how to analyze data from one or more single-system studies. The most common position and practice is to rely solely upon the visual interpretation of the data, observing clear trends, as in seeing if the data are clearly going up, going down, or not clearly chang-ing in either direction. In all but very definite changes, this may be difficult to determine. Thus, when you can see it, it is probably really there and not wishful thinking or bias on your part. To check, show your data to colleagues and ask for their judgments. This is, oddly enough, very much a qualitative appraisal. There are no clear decision rules to guide you, as there are in interpreting the results of an inferential statistic like a t-test. Thus, you will likely miss picking up on some real changes, real in the sense that a nonstatistically trivial change occurred. But such small effects, even though reliable, have traditionally been seen by ad-vocates of SSDs as not likely to be very practically important. This is especially true when your unit of analysis is an individual client as opposed to aggregate statistics from some much larger unit of investigation, such as statewide health statistics. A 5% reduction in AIDS mortality may be *really* important from a public health perspective, but a 5% reduction in a melancholic client's Beck Depression Inventory scores will not likely be significant, statistically or clinically. As mentioned earlier, relying solely upon visual interpretation of SSD data may increase the chance of committing a Type II research error (missing a true effect or what is called a *false negative*).

For certain types of SSDs, those involving very many data points per phase (say 50 or more), a highly specialized form of inferential statistic called time-series analysis can be judiciously applied to examine the significance of changes between phases, say, in an AB design. But such SSDs are relatively rare, with the large majority of SSDs having 10 or fewer data points per phase. Moreover, the use of time-series analysis is a pretty specialized technique, likely one you are not familiar with, and you may even have trouble finding someone locally who could help you run and interpret the analysis.

Some methodologically oriented social workers have advocated trying to apply conventional inferential statistics to SSD data. Their reasoning goes something like the following: the data in an A phase of an AB design can be treated as the pretreatment data of a nonexperimental pretest-posttest group design (described in the next chapter). If you had 10 data points on some outcome measure (dependent variable) that was scored on an interval or ratio scale, you could take the average (mean) and standard deviation of the A phase data and compare it to the mean data in the B phase. You could apply a paired-sample t-test to these data, just like you could if you had a small-group design, with 10 clients assessed before and after receiving a social work intervention. The result could tell you if the difference between the mean data in the A phase and B phase was statistically significantly different. Moreover, this type of analysis is capable of detecting smaller effects than you could determine through simply looking at the graphed data. Similarly, if you had an ABA or an ABAB design, you could use a one-by-three or one-by-four analysis of variance for repeated measures to look for data differences among more than two phases. If the data are scored using a categorical (yes or no, present or absent, positive or negative, etc.) or ordinal scale (e.g., not depressed, mildly depressed, very depressed), you could use certain nonparametric statistical tests, such as the chi-square analysis.

There are several reasons why such approaches are not widely used. One, and perhaps the least defensible, is that these suggestions do violence to the otherwise elegant simplicity of SSDs and may deter the statistically uninformed from attempting to evaluate their own practice using SSDs if their use was conflated with the concurrent necessity of mastering certain inferential statistics, something social workers may not be too adept at. But there are sounder reasons. Most examples of SSDs have 10 or fewer data points per phase. Yet the number of data points in a given phase of an SSD establishes the degrees of freedom used in the calculation of inferential tests of statistical significance. Most SSDs would have so few data points as to have a correspondingly low degree of freedom, and hence very low *statistical power*, that is, the ability to find an effect.

Another problem is that one of the major assumptions behind the proper use of most statistical tests is that the data are independent, which is a fancy way of saying that knowledge of one given data point does not help predict what the other data points' values will be. Now you can see how this assumption of independence would be true for, say, 20 clients recruited to participate in a pretest-posttest group design. A given person's score on some outcome measure is clearly unconnected with another person's score among these 20 people. *But,* in the case of a person who is the focus of an AB design, his or her score on one day will likely be related to his or her score on other days or weeks because you have a series of data points from the same person. This violates the assumption of the independence of the data that inferential tests are based upon. If the data are sufficiently so correlated, they display a statistical property called serial dependence (or autocorrelation), then the usual statistical tests of differences become invalid. As we noted, some tests take this dependence into account (e.g., a paired-samples t-test), but, by and large, most statisticians shudder at the idea of applying tests intended to look at group differences to the level of analyzing change within individual clients.

Another problem with most parametric inferential tests is that they look at the "average" data in a given phase and compare it to the average data in another phase. Such an analysis ignores the crucial variable of the data's *slope* completely. Suppose the A data in an AB design are descending and, in fact, getting worse, and the B data in the same client depict an immediate reversal of this trend, moving in the positive direction with an upward slope. It could turn out that the mean of the A phase data and the mean of the B phase data are exactly the same, and an inferential test would find out that there was absolutely no difference between the data in the A and B phases. In reality, the visual inspection of the data would reveal that the introduction of social work intervention, B, was immediately followed by a sharp and sustained improvement.

So, for the purposes of this book, you are urged to rely upon the visual inspection of graphically presented single-system data as your primary means of interpreting changes within and between phases. There are too many problems associated with using most statistical tests to warrant advocating them at this point. And it is worth reemphasizing that SSDs are almost never accompanied by the use of such tests. It is simply not common practice. For good reason.

We have long recognized that inferential and other statistical treatments are not necessary when conclusions are obvious. Almost 100 years ago, Kate Claghorn (1908) had this to say at a major social work conference:

> We should break off the habit of referring every question to statistical investigation as a matter of course; we should determine whether it is not sufficiently plain in its obvious aspects, so as to avoid resorting to a laborious process of proof of something quite well-known before. (p. 249)

Are there any decision rules you can follow when visually interpreting SSD data? Only a few simple ones:

- Just assume that if a change is not visually obvious, then no change occurred.

- Assume that if a change is visually obvious to you and to others, that change occurred.

- Look at the pattern of overlapping data points between adjacent phases. The more overlap, the less likely you have captured any real (e.g., practically important) changes. The less overlap, the better, and phases with no overlap are the most convincing evidence that the data are really different (e.g., that change occurred). This is especially true when you have lots of data points in each phase.

- Having more data points allows for clearer inferences than having just a few data points per phase. The fewer the number of data points, the more conservative you should be in making inferences regarding change.

HOW TO GRAPH DATA*

Although you can simply record your data from the SSD as a column of numbers, it is often difficult to visually detect changes within and between phases. The more common practice is to portray such data on a line graph. A line graph has two borders, a flat horizontal line from left to right used to depict the dimension of time, and a vertical line used to depict the client or system's scores on some outcome measures, with the two lines forming an L.

Here are some other general guidelines for use in preparing lines graphs depicting single-system data:

Things to Do

1. Use somewhat larger (i.e., thicker) lines to form the vertical and horizontal axes than those lines used to connect data points.

2. Use black ink only. Colored ink will not clearly reproduce on common black-and-white photocopiers.

3. Use actual data points (e.g., solid black circles, open black circles, etc.) connected by a line as opposed to a jerky line alone, lacking data points.

4. Separate phases using a dashed vertical line.

5. Label each phase with a brief, intelligible title (e.g., Baseline, Intervention, etc.).

6. Use abbreviations sparingly, or not at all. Spell out things if space permits.

7. Elevate the lowest value found on the vertical axis slightly above the horizontal axis so that data points do not rest upon it.

8. Make the graph big enough to read easily.

---

* Portions of this section are from Royse et al. (2006, p. 188).

Things Not to Do

1. Never use colored ink, and try not to use shades of gray as colors and shadings reproduce poorly when photocopied.

2. Do not format your graph using a computer's three-dimensional drawing feature. Although these may look prettier, they do so at the expense of being able to clearly tell where data falls along an axis.

3. If you are submitting your report for publication in a professional journal, do not include a figure caption on the figure itself. Use a separate figure caption page as required by the style set for in the *Publication Manual of the American Psychological Association*.

4. Do not have a top or a right-hand border on the graph.

5. Do not use horizontal lines running from the vertical axis across the graph.

6. Do not connect data points between phases. Instead, have a break in the data.

It may be helpful to include in your graphs lines depicting the means and slopes of the data within each phase as an aid to the visual inspection of the data (see Fisher, Kelley, & Lomas, 2003; Normand & Bailey, 2006; Stocks & Williams, 1995).

There are a number of tutorials available to help you construct such line graphs using commonly available word processing and graphing programs (see Carr & Burkholder, 1998; Grehan & Moran, 2005; Moran & Hirschbine, 2002), and one group of social work faculty has prepared specialized software to do the same thing (see Conboy, Auerbach, Beckerman, Schnall, & LaPorte, 2000). This program also incorporates certain inferential statistical tests and is more extensively elaborated upon in Bloom et al. (2006). Such programs are very useful in preparing professional-looking line graphs and are highly recommended, as is social worker Mark Mattaini's (1993) terrific book *More Than a Thousand Words: Graphs for Clinical Practice*.

OBSTACLES TO USING SSDs

You may be thinking that using SSDs to help you in evaluating the outcomes of your own practice or your agency's programs may not be very practical or that you may lack the time, expertise, resources, or administrative support to do this. To some extent, we respond to such concerns by pointing out that, as the examples in this chapter demonstrate, social workers, including students, can and do use these in a wide array of practice settings. Internationally, SSDs have also been widely applied. British social worker Mansoor Kazi has collaborated with human service practitioners to produce literally hundreds of SSDs, many of which have been published (e.g., Kazi, 1998; Kazi & Wilson, 1996). Social workers have also had great success in using SSDs in Finland (e.g., Kazi, Mantysaari, & Rostila, 1997), and their applications in China have also been described (Thyer, Artelt, & Shek, 2003). So it is not so much a question of can they be used since the answer to that is yes.

The question of time is a legitimate one, and overburdened, underpaid social workers with huge caseloads may honestly feel that they simply cannot do this for reasons of insufficient time. And, frankly, they may be right. If you really can't, then don't, and don't fret about it. We are certainly not arguing that you must use these designs with every client you see nor have we argued that social workers should be required to use these designs. Rather, we have laid out guidelines for how to use them and how they may prove useful. If you found this information interesting and applicable, then great, we have done our job. You might also take the perspective that perhaps, just perhaps, there will be the occasional client or situation you encounter wherein these SSDs might be applicable. If so, you could take them for a test drive, so to speak. We recommend starting simple, trying to apply a B or AB design rather than one of the more complex designs at first. If this proves successful and useful, you will be encouraged to try again and perhaps eventually have an opportunity to apply a more stringent method.

We also note that these designs do not really take as much time as you perhaps anticipate. Most social workers are already spending considerable efforts in assessing clients and maybe in evaluating outcomes less formally than we have described in this chapter. Asking clients to complete one RAI a week and then scoring it and plotting it on a piece of graph paper or on a computer-generated graph takes but a few minutes a week at best. Think small, think practical. At least initially.

Agency support is of course really nice to have. If you show your supervisor an AB chart of one of your cases with positive results, and she or he responds enthusiastically, encourages you to continue, and holds up your fine work as an exemplar for the other social workers in your agency, you are truly among the blessed. If this happens, great, but don't count on it. You may need to seek out alternative sources of reinforcement. Client feedback about how helpful and encouraging it is for them to review their graphs with you is one possible source. Peer feedback can be another. Presenting your SSD cases at the monthly meetings of the local chapter of the National Association of Social Workers (NASW) or the Clinical Social Work Association or at a state, regional, or national conference can be especially gratifying. Many associations' conferences allow poster presentations in lieu of presenting a formal, oral paper, and this can be a very nonintimidating way to introduce yourself to this type of public presentation of your work. And many journals welcome the submission of SSDs for possible publication, which is perhaps one of the strongest reinforcers of all. Section 5.01(d) of the NASW's *Code of Ethics* clearly states:

> Social workers should contribute to the knowledge base of social work and share with colleagues their knowledge related to practice, research, and ethics. Social workers should seek to contribute to the profession's literature and to share their knowledge at professional meetings and conferences. (NASW, 1999, p. 24)

We would also like to note that, although the examples provided in this chapter on the use of SSDs to evaluate practice have focused upon their applications at the level of direct practice, they may also be used to evaluate social work interventions provided on larger scales such as community practice or even the evaluation of social welfare policies (see Thyer, 1998, 2006).

SUMMARY

Single-system designs are an extremely versatile method for social workers to use in evaluating their own practice and agency-based programs. The level of system being evaluated dictates your choice of outcome measures, but the inferential logic of these designs remains the same whether your unit of analysis is a single person, a couple, a family, a small group, an organization, a city, state, or an entire country. If some suitable outcome measure assessing the functioning or status of your client can be credibly assessed repeatedly over time, you can make use of SSDs. These have been and remain widely used to examine the outcomes of our services and have appeared in all our field's major practice and research journals.

4

Group Evaluation Designs

GENERAL PRINCIPLES AND NOTATION

You will recall that SSDs usually involve taking systematic measures of some outcome measure many times for a very small number of clients or systems. GRDs take another approach, taking systematic measures of some outcome measure only one, two, or a very few times, but with a large number of clients. Like SSDs, GRDs can be arranged along a hierarchy of designs, ranging from those very weak in internal validity (e.g., they do not usually permit the practitioner to make any legitimate causal inferences) to those with potentially very strong internal validity. Regrettably, those GRDs that are the most practical to implement, pose the least intrusions into the delivery of service, are the most acceptable to clients, and present the least potential ethical problems, are the designs of weaker internal validity. Nevertheless, conducting even simple GRDs is a useful practice for most social workers to attempt and can have practical applications.

GRDs have their own schematic notation or way to be diagramed. Systematic assessments made of outcome measures are usually referred to as *pretreatment measurements* or an observational phase of a study. This part of a GRD is abbreviated with an O, indicating an observational phase. The period of time during which treatment is provided is abbreviated with an X. Thus, for example, an O-X-O design refers to a pretreatment assessment made of a group of clients who then received treatment. Following treatment, they were assessed again using the selected outcome measure. Following this terminology, an O-X-O-O design would indicate that a second posttreatment assessment was undertaken, perhaps to measure any changes some time later, to see if initial improvements were maintained, or to see if an initial period of no improvement was followed by subsequent changes. We will further explore this notational system as this chapter progresses.

SAMPLING

Most research textbooks in social work and other disciplines take up a large amount of space explaining various ways social workers can obtain samples of clients. Usually there is great stress laid on the importance of trying to obtain what is called a probability (or representative) sample of clients. If one can do this, then it is claimed that the findings from the sample (deemed representative of a larger population of interest) may be generalizable to that population. For example, if a social work intervention is found to be highly helpful for a randomly selected sample of clients with a particular problem, say, major depression, then it is hoped that the treatment would also be effective for other persons with depression—those not included in the sample. Such considerations are, of course, important to promote the development of social work as a science-based discipline whose results are not idiosyncratic to specific times, places, clients, or service providers. Obtaining a true random sample of clients is more feasible with certain forms of research than others. For example, a study using a mailed survey to examine the social service needs of adult clients in a given community may be able to use census records, voter registration roles, or telephone directories to develop something very close to a representative group of people to invite to participate in the study.

But other forms of research rely much less heavily on trying to obtain a representative sample of clients from which to generalize findings, For example, many forms of qualitative research make no pretense at trying to establish the generalizability of the findings, with the researchers being content to make inferences limited to only those participants who were studied. The evaluation of the outcomes of social work practice is another form of research that is primarily oriented to evaluating how a given agency's clients fared following treatment or, at the level of the individual practitioners, it is oriented to answering the limited question of "How did *my* clients do following receipt of my services?" Evaluations of such focused scope should not be sneered at as simple administrative exercises or of limited scientific value. The fact of the matter is that, when it comes to conducting evaluations of social work practice, there are almost no published examples that successfully obtained a true and complete probability sample. In fact, we, the authors, know of none. The reality is that almost all efforts to date on evaluating social work practice have made use of what can be called samples of convenience or samples of ready availability, most often consisting of clients seen at one or more agencies that administrators gave the social work researchers access to.

Sometimes, the sample size of published studies can be impressively large, but recall from your introduction to research class the fundamental fact that, unless a sample has been obtained through genuine random selection, one may not generalize the findings from that sample to a larger population *no matter how large the sample*. There is a sort of intuitive sense that a nonrandom sample of 100 clients has the potential to yield findings that are inherently more generalizable to a larger population of interest than a similarly nonrandom sample of, say, only 50 clients or 25 participants. But our intuition is wrong here. An atypical sample remains atypical (e.g., nonrepresentative) no matter how impressively large. Thus, the large-scale, federally funded outcome study using a nonrandom sample of clients in New York City is no more generalizable to other clients than the small-scale outcome study conducted by social workers at the local family service agency in rural Georgia. Now, to be sure, the larger-size outcome investigation, with appropriate control groups, may be a more *internally valid* study in that its conclusions related to causal inference may be stronger, but the *external validity* may be equally compromised in both large- and small-scale efforts that employed nonprobability sampling methods.

This is by way of encouraging you, the social worker reading this book, to not feel that your efforts to evaluate your own practice outcomes or those of your agencies are of little use in terms of advancing our field. Most practitioners, and most agencies for that matter, have little systematic, reliable, and credible evidence regarding the client outcomes of the services they provide. Undertaking such efforts is a form of personal professional development, is ethically appropriate, and may result in findings that can be of practical value to you and your agency.

GRDs can be conceptualized along the following three questions:

1. Are pretreatment assessments made of the outcome measures before treatment begins?

2. Are various control groups used? (If the answer is yes, then you have a quasi-experimental or experimental design.)

3. Are the various groups or conditions participants are assigned to constructed using random assignment methods? (If the answer is yes, then you have an experimental design.)

These different types of GRDs are described and illustrated below.

PREEXPERIMENTAL DESIGNS

The preexperimental GRDs have a tremendously valuable role to play in the evaluation of social work practice. They are the simplest, least costly, least intrusive, and easiest to understand of all the nomothetic approaches. By the term *preexperimental*, all that is meant is that the results usually do not, no matter how apparently clear, permit the social worker or the reader to draw any legitimate causal inferences regarding the effects of treatment. In other words, they are not very good at answering the question, "Did my treatment cause the clients to get better?" But they are often quite good at answering the question, "Did my clients get better?" and this is an enormously useful thing to know.

The One-Group Posttest-Only Design

The simplest of the preexperimental designs is called the *one-group posttest-only design*. This approach involves selecting one or more reliable and valid outcome measures relevant to your clients' condition and then assessing them using this measure at some point after they have received social work services, usually after services have ended. Schematically, this design is diagramed as X-O, with X indicating a period of time when clients were receiving services and O as the observational phase wherein the outcome measure was administered. The use of more than one outcome measure is, of course, possible. Ideally, this design is used when you have a sizable number of clients with the *same problem* and who received the *same services*. This is often only a subset of an agency's clients or of the variety of the services provided, but restricting the design in this manner makes for the "cleanest" outcome study. You can, of course, lump clients with many differing problems or circumstances and who received many and varying types of social work services together into a single X-O design, but this will likely not be as helpful.

Say, for example, you had several social workers providing various forms of continuing education workshops: some on the treatment of disparate mental disorders, others on supervision, others on state-mandated ethics training, and so forth. At the conclusion of each workshop, participants were asked to complete an evaluation form relating to the continuing education program they just attended. If all the trainers' course evaluations for all the workshops, some with differing subject matter, were grouped together, and assuming you used a "good" measure to evaluate the training sessions, you could calculate an omnibus satisfaction rating, one that combines the training provided by all workers in many different content areas. You can see how it would be more useful to list each workshop's results separately, broken down by who provided the training and the subject matter. It may be that Mr. Jones's workshop on clinical supervision gets the consistently lowest course evaluations. This useful information would be obscured if Jones's course evaluations were combined with those of all the other trainers.

The X-O design is especially useful in conducting client-satisfaction studies or in appraisals of services wherein there were no measures of pretreatment functioning. One of the authors, Laura Myers, used this type of design in her doctoral dissertation. Laura found that there are very few follow-up studies on the adult psychosocial functioning and well-being of individuals who had been raised in a traditional orphanage, an institutional group-home environment where biological or sociological "orphans" are permanently placed with no subsequent efforts made for their permanent adoption or foster care in a more conventional family. Although the child welfare system has officially adopted the position that adoption or foster care are preferable alternatives to placement in traditional orphanages, orphanages have always been a significant resource for the placement of children, and they continue to be so today.

Laura knew the pastor associated with a traditional orphanage in Florida, one with a long history and run by a Protestant denomination, and was able to use this connection to gain access. After getting her university's Human Protection Review Committee's approval for the project, Laura obtained a mailing list of all alumni who had been raised in this orphanage. She prepared a survey packet of several standardized measures of psychosocial functioning (e.g., life satisfaction, quality of life, etc.) and an original questionnaire asking them about their experiences at the orphanage and current life circumstances (marital status, socioeconomic status, educational level, etc.). The packets were mailed by the director of the orphanage, along with a postpaid return envelope and a cover letter from the director asking the alumni to complete the forms and return them to the orphanage. The director in turn gave them to Laura.

The results, analyzed primarily descriptively, found that the large majority of the participants expressed positive views about their life in the orphanage, had favorable recollections about the quality of the care they received, and had fared well, on average, in terms of social and economic success—better, in fact, than would be expected according to national norms. This research approach made use of the X-O, one-group posttest-only design and was perfectly appropriate to answer the questions being posed. The results were published in respectable social work and human service journals (see Myers & Rittner, 1999; Myers & Rittner, 2001).

Many published examples of the X-O design are available. Bruce Thyer used this approach in his initial effort to evaluate a method of college teaching, one that involved having students complete weekly written responses to comprehensive study questions based on that week's assigned readings. He used this in a number of BSW, MSW, and PhD social work courses and, at the conclusion of each, asked the students to anonymously complete an evaluation form asking for their agreement or disagreement to statements such as: "I found answering the study questions a better learning tool than having to write a term paper," "Answering the study questions helped me to keep up to date in my readings," "I found answering the study questions an excellent way to learn the course content," and so forth. The results of the student evaluations indicated that using weekly written study questions was very favorably appraised by the students (see Thyer, 1988) and a later study of nine other social work classes, using the X-O design and taught by other faculty who used this approach, corroborated the initial results (see Thyer, Sutphen, & Sowers-Hoag, 1990). Another social worker, Jan Ligon, who was an administrator of a large mental health system in Atlanta used the X-O design to conduct a consumer satisfaction study of a crisis stabilization program provided to individuals with a serious mental illness or substance abuse problem and their families. This study, involving the real-life recipients of community mental health services, had 54 clients and 29 family members provide client satisfaction ratings using a reliable and valid measure (see Ligon & Thyer, 2000a).

This simple X-O design can also be useful to screen out *ineffective* interventions. If an intervention does not survive being appraised in this manner (e.g., the instruction is negatively evaluated or the practice outcomes are very poor), then a social worker may judge that something needs to be changed, and perhaps discontinue something that is not working very well. This can be a good thing. Social work MSW intern Grace Sutherland conducted a follow-up assessment of human service providers, attempting to see if the workers had implemented the training they had received in developing linkages between the developmental disability and geronto-logical service communities. Sadly, this proved to rarely be the case, according to the results of a telephone survey of 64 randomly selected participants. This stimulated the provider of these continuing educational workshops to implement additional efforts to promote coalition building between these two groups of professionals (see Sutherland-Smith, Thyer, Clements, & Kropf, 1997).

In contrast, MSW intern Wendy Pabian conducted a follow-up evaluation of clients at a comprehensive diagnostic center serving families of children with devel-opmental disabilities to empirically ascertain the extent to which these families had availed themselves of the services recommended by the program. Some four months after the evaluations and treatment recommendations had been completed, 36 fami-lies were contacted, and it was found that a very large proportion of the educational and treatment recommendations had been acted upon. Given that the purpose of Wendy's agency was to provide these families with such recommendations, it was a very good thing indeed to find out that they were being followed by the families (see Pabian, Thyer, Straka, & Boyle, 2000).

Pretest-Posttest One-Group Design

An advance over the X-O design is to use some sort of pretreatment or pretest measurement of one's clients, creating what is called the *pretest-posttest one-group design*, diagramed as an O-X-O study. This approach can be used to answer ques-tions like "Did clients who received this intervention get better, on average?" One is in a better position to judge *improvements* among a group of participants (ide-ally clients with the same problem who received the same intervention) using a pretest assessment. Usually with simple inferential statistics such as a t-test (for interval or ratio-scaled outcome measures) or chi-square test (for categorical or ordinal scaled measures), one can compare the difference between the scores be-fore and after intervention.

This approach was used by John Buchanan (Buchanan, Dixon, & Thyer, 1997), an MSW intern assigned to an inpatient psychiatry program at a veterans' hospital. John and his field instructor, Danny Dixon, knew that there was little evidence beyond the level of clinical anecdote and impression that patients treated on this unit improved. Sadly, the same situation often prevails at many social service agencies. With the approval of the hospital's research review committee, they arranged for newly admitted patients to be given a reliable and valid measure of psychiatric symptomatology shortly after admission and again shortly before planned discharge. This was done for a total of 30 patients treated and discharged within a three-month period. The average length of stay was 22 days, and all met the criteria for a serious mental illness. It was found that statistically significant and important improvements were reported on all of the outcome measure's subscales as appraised by t-tests. This was a good thing to find. Imagine if it was found that there had been no improvements or that the patients, on average, had gotten worse. In some ways, conducting simple evaluations like this is a brave undertaking because it exposes a social service program to the risk of documenting negative outcomes. (We suspect that one reason why agencies do not conduct outcome evaluations more often is to avoid this risk.)

John and Danny were very cautious in the claims they made in their report, appropriately noting that:

> This type of design is effective at answering the question "Do patients improve?", but is not usually useful in proving that a given treatment *caused* [italics in original] any observed improvements. Given that most VA psychiatric services have no data to document simple improvements, it is suitable to begin evaluation research looking at outcomes alone, before undertaking the more sophisticated studies needed to isolate causal variables. (p. 856)

So long as you do not succumb to the understandable (but not scientifically legitimate) temptation to claim that the O-X-O design with favorable results *proved* your services are effective, then you are on solid ground to claim that your clients got better, again assuming that you have a reliable and valid outcome measure.

The O-X-O design is an extensively used approach to clinical and program evaluation. It does not require large groups of participants, withholding of treatment from anyone, or that potential participants be randomly assigned to differing treatment conditions. Other examples of social workers using this design can be found in Robinson, Powers, Cleveland, and Thyer (1990); Gerardot, Thyer, Mabe, and Posten (1992); Carrillo, Gallant, and Thyer (1993); Capp, Thyer, and Bordnick (1997); Crolley, Roys, Thyer, and Bordnick, (1998); Schwartz and Thyer (2000); and Ligon and Thyer (2000b). It is worth noting that *every one* of the studies listed in this paragraph was undertaken by a social work *student*.

QUASI-EXPERIMENTAL DESIGNS

Although it is very nice to be able to provide credible data that one's clients have improved, occasionally social workers need to demonstrate not only that clients have gotten better, but also that they have strong reason to believe that the reason clients improved was the intervention they received from the social worker or the social worker's agency. Rubin and Babbie (2005) claim that "perhaps the most pressing causal issue facing today's social work profession concerns the effectiveness of social work services. What effects, if any, are *caused* [italics in original] by social workers?" (p. 314).

We believe that this is a correct assertion, and one approach to try to find out if improvements are caused by social workers is to conduct a more rigorous type of research design using what are called *quasi-experimental* designs. Quasi-experimental designs differ from preexperimental ones in that, apart from the group of participants receiving a given treatment of interest, there are also one or more groups of participants who either receive no treatment, alternative treatment, treatment as usual (TAU), or a placebo treatment (rarely found in social work outcome studies). By comparing the results of the clients who received a given treatment of interest with those who received something else or nothing, it may be possible to make some conclusions regarding the real effects of the treatment of interest. Usually, these comparison conditions arise naturally or in the given course of the provision of services. They are not usually developed by the social worker using artificial or contrived means. Here are some examples that will help illustrate these designs.

The simplest quasi-experimental group design can be called the *posttest-only comparison group design*, which can be diagramed as follows:

$$X \quad O$$
$$O$$

Here, one group of people with a particular problem has received a social work intervention (labeled X) and, afterward, is assessed or observed using a reliable and valid outcome measure (labeled O). At the same time the treatment group is assessed, another group of people who have the same type of problem, but did not receive the treatment (X), is also assessed. If the treatment group is doing much better (usually determined via inferential statistical tests examining posttreatment functioning of the treatment group compared to the no-treatment group), one's grounds for inferring the beneficial effects of treatment are a bit stronger than is usually possible with the preexperimental designs. The confidence of such a conclusion is dependent upon several factors: the determination that any differences are indeed statistically significant and clinically meaningful, the lability of the clients' problem (or the extent to which it can be expected to naturally wax and wane in severity), the reliability and validity of the outcome measure, and so on. For a problem known to be persistent and severe, assessed with a strong outcome measure, and with robust statistical effects, one might be pretty confident that social work intervention caused the treated group to improve. But such judgments are, to some extent, a judgment call—what Shadish et al. (2002) call "fuzzy plausibility" (p. 484).

Instead of a group of clients who did not receive treatment, one may compare clients who received a targeted intervention to people who received another intervention, to sham therapy, or to treatment as usual. One such design might be diagramed as follows:

$$X \quad O$$
$$Y \quad O$$
$$O$$

In this design, one group receives a novel intervention (X), another group receives treatment as usual (Y), and a third receives no treatment. These designs, like all approaches to measuring the outcomes of practice, can be strengthened by repeating posttreatment assessments sometime after the initial one conducted immediately after treatment. This might be as follows:

$$X \quad O \quad O$$
$$Y \quad O \quad O$$

Such follow-up assessments are useful to see if any differences between the two groups immediately posttreatment are maintained at follow-up (say, some three or six months later). Or the groups might have been equivalent immediately posttreatment, but, at follow-up, one group may have improved or deteriorated relative to the clients in the other condition. Here are some real-life examples of using quasi experiments to look at the outcomes of social work.

MSW intern Emily Gary was assigned to a prenatal care program that provided services to high-risk, low-income women living in rural Georgia. The prenatal care team drove in a van to identified rural counties and provided prenatal care services to pregnant women. Over the course of the program, some of the clients ended up making almost all of their appointments, and others ended up missing quite a few. Emily identified the top 25% of those women who kept almost all their appointments and thereby received the most amount of prenatal care and the bottom 25% of the appointment keepers enrolled in the program who got the least amount of care. Thus, the patients were divided into two groups without any contrivance on the part of the Emily or the other members of the prenatal care team. Emily examined the patient records of all women in the program who had their babies during a given six-month period and looked at a number of perinatal outcome measures. This quasi-experimental posttest-only comparison groups design could be diagrammed as follows:

$$X \quad O$$
$$Y \quad O$$

X was the women who made most (13 or more) of their appointments ($N=27$) and Y represented those who made very few (four or less) of their appointments ($N=28$). Emily found that the women who made most of their appointments had babies that weighed statistically significantly more than the babies whose moms made few appointments, and they also had babies with longer gestational ages. There are also barely nonsignificant trends for the babies of high-attending moms to have higher Apgar scores (a test of the baby's success in adapting to the extrauterine environment) than the babies born of the low-attending mothers. These are good results: ones you would hope to see from an effective program of prenatal care. This was a risky study for Emily and the prenatal care team to undertake. Suppose they had found out that there were absolutely no differences in birth outcomes? That would have been a pretty damning indictment of the effectiveness of the prenatal care program. Emily was appropriately cautious in her conclusion:

> The lack of a true experimental design incorporating random assignment to high and low numbers of appointments precludes a completely uncritical acceptance of the conclusion that these services are unambiguously effective. . . However, our findings are consistent with the hypothesis that routine prenatal care services provided to high-risk women are effective in improving perinatal birth outcomes. (Gary-McCormick, Thyer, Panton, & Myers, 2000, p. 56)

Can we be pretty *certain* that prenatal care helps moms give birth to fewer premature babies (e.g., give birth earlier to babies who weigh less)? Not really—not on the basis of this one study. But the evidence points in that direction, and it is always a good thing to have the evidence in your favor. It beats the alternative. Here are some other illustrations of quasi-experimental designs used by social workers.

Students who graduate with a BSW from a program accredited by the Council on Social Work Education may qualify for what is called "advanced standing," whereby if they enroll in an MSW program, they may be exempted from taking many of the foundation classes usually completed during the first year of MSW education. It is assumed that this curriculum content would have been covered during the BSW program. The granting of advanced standing was initially a controversial policy within the social work academic community, with some educators contending that was not warranted. To this day, MSW programs within the state of California do not permit advanced standing. BSWs applying to California MSW programs must complete the entire two-year traditional program of study. Social work faculty member and doctoral student Dorothy Carrillo was in the position of teaching the second-year MSW class, Theories of Social Work Practice. This class was being taken by newly admitted advanced-standing students (those with a BSW) and by MSW students without the BSW, who had completed the first year of the MSW and were now entering their second year. An important assignment of this class was to help assess and develop the students' clinical interviewing skills, and, at the beginning of the semester, all students completed a videotaped interview with a standardized mock client (role-played by one of the authors, Laura Myers). Dorothy wanted to empirically test the hypothesis that advanced-standing students' initial interviewing skills (as assessed at the beginning of her course) were equivalent to those of the students who had just completed the first year of their MSW program. Dorothy located a previously published, reliable and valid way to assess clinical interviewing skills (measuring the dimensions of facilitation, questioning or clarification, and empathy or support), as judged by two independent raters (themselves MSWs). These ratings were based on the judges watching the videotapes independently of each other and scoring the students' skills at interviewing.

As it naturally turned out, without any manipulation on Dorothy's part, she had 15 advanced-standing students and 23 traditional MSW students in her class. Her design could be diagrammed as:

$$X \qquad O$$
$$\text{-----------}$$
$$Y \qquad O$$

X represented the advanced-standing students with a BSW and newly starting the MSW program; Y represented the students who just completed the first year of the two-year MSW program; O was the judges' ratings of the student's interviewing skills; and the line separating the groups indicated that the groups were composed using methods other than random assignment. Also, it is worth noting that the raters of the videotapes did not know if the student whose clinical interviewing skills they were evaluating was an advanced-standing MSW student or a traditional MSW student. Having the raters work without knowing the students' status helped control for any biases the raters may have had with respect to the advanced-standing policy.

The results showed that the two groups of students *did not* differ in their clinical interviewing skills at the beginning of this advanced practice class. As Dorothy concluded (again conservatively):

> Results of the study were consistent with the hypothesis that equivalency between groups in the use of interviewing skills would be demonstrated. These findings support the appropriateness of the advanced standing policy and the practice of exempting qualified BSW students from portions of the MSW foundation coursework. There are, however, certain limitations of the results of this research. Chief among these is the low internal validity of the design. . . the findings cannot be interpreted to mean that all foundation content was comparably mastered by both groups. (Carrillo & Thyer, 1994, p. 385)

Was this a perfect study in terms of internal validity? Far from it. Was it adequate to answer Dorothy's major question, namely, do these two groups of students display equivalent interviewing skills? Yes, it was. Also, it is worth noting that Dorothy received approval to conduct this study from the university's IRB.

The identical design, with a different outcome measure, was used by social work students Betsy Vonk and Cindy Tandy in another test of how advanced-standing students compared to traditional MSW students. At the beginning of the second year of the MSW program of study 20 advanced-standing students (newly admitted into the MSW program) and 32 traditional program students (without a BSW and having just completed the first year of the MSW curriculum) took the practice examination used to license BSWs in those few states that actually legally regulate the practice of social work at the BSW level. This practice examination was a previously published 50-item multiple-choice test said to be identical in content and difficulty to the "real" test taken by BSWs seeking licensure. This designed looked like this:

$$X \quad O$$

$$Y \quad O$$

In this design, X represented the 20 advanced-standing students, Y the 32 traditional students, and O the average score on this practice examination. Once again, it was found that the two groups scored equivalently on this particular outcome measure, further supporting the policy of granting advanced standing to BSW students. This study, too, was approved by the university's IRB (see Thyer, Vonk, & Tandy, 1996).

A last example of the posttest-only comparison group design was used by social work student Betsy Vonk. There has been some discussion in the professional literature about the role of supervisor gender in terms of its relationship to the satisfaction supervisees have regarding the supervision they receive. Bluntly put, do women supervisees prefer to be supervised by women or by men and vice versa for male supervisees? If such influences exist, should they help determine the placement of social work students with potential field instructors or supervisors? After getting university IRB approval, Betsy mailed two previously published and validated measures of satisfaction with a clinical supervisor to all MSW students in their final semester of field placement. A total of 78 female MSW students responded (there were too few male students to analyze the data), of whom 60 were supervised by female field instructors and 18 by males. Thus, the students were naturally sorted (by their choosing course sections) into the following design:

$$X \quad O$$

$$Y \quad O$$

Here, X represented female MSW students with female supervisors, and Y represented female MSW students with male supervisors. O represented their group's average scores on satisfaction with supervision. Bottom line, no meaningful differences were found in the students' level of satisfaction with supervision, suggesting that the gender of the supervisor is not an important factor in one's satisfaction with supervision. If there had been large differences, then consideration might need to be given to a gender-matching policy in regard to the placement of students, but the absence of such apparent effects renders such a discussion moot (see Vonk, Zucrow, & Thyer, 1996). That this study's findings of a noneffect of supervisor gender replicated an earlier one that included male students as well as female students also suggests that a gender-matching policy of student to field instructor is not warranted (Thyer, Sowers-Hoag, & Love, 1986). This latter study had a quasi-experimental posttest-only comparison design with four groups (male student with male supervisor, etc.).

Quasi-experimental designs may be strengthened by including pretreatment assessments for each naturally occurring group, as well as the posttreatment assessment described above. This could be diagramed as follows:

The merits of such pretreatment assessments is that they allow you to empirically examine whether the groups are equivalent on demographic and outcome measures before social work intervention. If they are really similar pretreatment, and there are significant differences evident posttreatment, one has stronger grounds (but still shaky) to assert that the various interventions experienced (or not experienced as in a no-treatment comparison group) by the two groups caused these differences in outcomes. This was the approach used by the productive Betsy Vonk for her doctoral dissertation. Betsy was a LCSW employed at the student counseling center at Emory University. The center had an interdisciplinary staff and saw students with a wide array of problems. Each individual therapist also tended to use his or her own approach to therapy (e.g., some used behavioral methods, others cognitive-behavioral, others psychodynamic, etc.), a situation common to many outpatient mental health clinics. Another commonality was that sometimes, when a student showed up seeking help, each of the therapists had a full caseload, and the new applicant for counseling was placed on a waiting list to be seen when an opening developed among one of the therapists. It was the usual practice at this counseling center to administer to each student seeking help a previously published, standardized, reliable, and valid measure of psychological symptoms. This was given at intake and at termination. For students placed on the waiting list, they completed it at intake, then again some time later when they actually began counseling, and then a third time at termination. This naturally occurring situation set the stage for Betsy to insert the data into the configuration of a quasi-experimental pretest-posttest delayed treatment comparison group design, something that could be diagramed as follows:

The top group represented students seen right away for counseling, and the bottom group represented those who were placed on a waiting list before beginning counseling. The line separating the two groups reflects the fact that they were not composed using random assignment.

The results were both interesting and favorable to the counseling center. Both groups of students were shown to have equivalent levels of psychological symptoms at intake. The top group of students, those who received immediate treatment (*N*=41), displayed statistically significant and important improvements right after treatment. This is good. The bottom group (*N*=14) had basically no changes in students' levels of psychological symptoms from their first and second administrations of the outcome measure. This was bad for them (they were still suffering), but good for Betsy and the counseling center, and it meant that the students' problems did not tend to go away on their own simply because of the passage of time. This bottom group's two assessments in effect represents a no-treatment comparison group condition and corroborates the hypothesis that the counseling was helpful and more so than simply waiting. Then, when the second group received counseling, on the third assessment, the students then experienced significant improvements equal to those seen among the students who got into treatment immediately. This, in effect, was a replicated finding that getting formal counseling was followed by improvements. This was good for Betsy and her colleagues (see Vonk and Thyer, 1999).

It is worth pointing out that this quasi-experimental design cost Betsy very little. The measures were already being gathered by the agency, the clients were already being seen, and all that was required of her was to exhort her colleagues to be sure to administer the outcome measures as per agency policy and to enter the data into a database and analyze it. Betsy found very few empirical program evaluations of university student counseling centers, hundreds of which can be found across the United States and for which there is little evidence that they actually help students. This study, in many ways so methodologically primitive, actually represented, at the time it was published, the most sophisticated outcome study ever conducted on university student counseling centers, again demonstrating the value of quasi-experimental designs in terms of adding to the evidence-based foundations of a given field. It also served as Betsy's successfully defended doctoral dissertation in social work, another substantial benefit to her.

A final example of a quasi experiment presented in this chapter can be diagramed as follows:

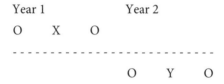

Year 1   Year 2
O   X   O

- -

              O   Y   O

Can you figure out what this means? Social worker Tracy Carpenter-Aeby was employed at an alternative school, a separate and specialized program for chronically disruptive youths. Such alternative schools attempt to provide a place for students to receive intensive social, educational, and behavioral services to prevent school dropout. Students are "assigned" to an alternative school for periods of time ranging from 45 to 180 school days. It is hoped that students will experience improvements in grades, comportment, self-esteem, the desire to drop out, depression, and other psychosocial variables. Upon entry to the alternative school, students are assessed on a number of these variables, some of which involve standardized, previously published measures known to be reliable and valid, (i.e., those related to self-esteem, depression, and locus of control), while others are more idiosyncratic (e.g., grades and attendance). These were reassessed at discharge. Grades and attendance were assessed based upon the student's performance during his or her most recently completed academic term in their regular school, after release from the alternative school (AS) and resumption of regular schooling, and again for the first completed academic term post-AS.

Following the completion of one academic year, it was administratively decided that, during the following academic year, the AS would implement a new feature among its services, namely, an added intensive program of family group work to be coordinated by the social worker, Tracy. This program of intensive family involvement included about one hour for every 15 days of school of family participation in staff meetings, other family counseling sessions ranging in intensity from three to 28 hours per family, phone conferences with the family (ranging from two to 11 a term, averaging once a week), a minimum of eight hours of family therapy, family meetings called as needed, family-teacher conferences (one to five per term), ad hoc meetings with staff and family as required, and transitional meetings aimed at helping the student reenter the regular school system. During this second year, students received an average of 44 hours of family-focused services compared to about 18 hours of such services the prior year. Keep in mind that these two years involved different cohorts of students. It was hypothesized that intensive family services during the second year of this study would result in greater improvements than those seen during the first year. The protocol for this study was approved by the university IRB, as well as by the local school system.

Thus, in the design diagramed above, the top group represents the first year's student cohort: 95 students seen during the 1994–1995 school year. The bottom group represents the second year wherein intensive family services were provided to augment the AS program. This took place during 1995–1996 and consisted of 120 students. Both groups were assessed at the beginning and at discharge from the AS during both years. What were the results? Well, not as positive as Tracy had hoped. Neither self-esteem, depression, nor locus of control enhancements were greater during the second year when intensive family services were provided. However, the students in the second year, who received intensive family services experienced statistically significantly greater improvements in grade point averages and in attendance and decreased dropout rates compared to the cohort that received the standard AS program the prior year. These are important and positive enhancements. While it is of course tempting to claim that adding intensive family services was causally linked to these improvements, Tracy and her colleagues conservatively noted the following:

The nonrandom nature of assigning students to the two programs makes causal inferences problematic, a common failing in field-based, naturalistic research studies conducted within the context of providing regular educational programming. (Aeby, Manning, Thyer, & Carpenter-Aeby, 1999, p. 29)

Now the astute reader will have noticed that, while quasi-experimental GRDs are usually a decided advance over the use of preexperimental designs, in almost every case the authors hedge their bets, saying something like, "While our results are consistent with the hypothesis that treatment X helped out clients, we really can't say that this is true with any certainty." And, as repeatedly noted, this is appropriately conservative in a scientific sense. In order to make more confident assertions such as, "Yes, by God, I have *proved* that treatment X *caused* the noted improvements!" one must usually employ the next most rigorous type of GRD—*genuine experiments.*

EXPERIMENTAL DESIGNS

True GRD experiments differ from quasi experiments through their conscious use of one very important methodological advance, namely, the random assignment of clients to various control groups. Via the magic of random assignment, you can be virtually certain that your groups are equivalent on just about any variable you can conceive of: those related to client demographics, those related to outcome measures, severity of client problems, client strengths, astrological sign, and so on. Thus, with some assurance that the client groups were the same *before* treatment, you can have greater confidence that any posttreatment differences are really because of the different treatment experiences they were assigned to.

The value of experimentation has long been recognized in social work. Frank Bruno (1936) made the following statements in his influential book, *The Theory of Social Work:*

On the one side, as scientists, we must believe that the curious medley of behaviors which together go make this complex world of ours, with its satisfactions and disappointments, is caused. We cannot accept the hypothesis of a blind fate or chance. There is this sense in this business of living, and consequently if we were wise enough, that we should be able to understand it, and, eventually, set up some sort of control over it. That is the implied objective of all social research. This brings us back to the one refuge offered us by the social scientists, and more particularly by the social philosophers: experimentation with its pragmatic principles. All advances in social work so far have been made by experiment. (p. 589)

A few years earlier, the influential social work educator Edith Abbot (1931) made an even bolder assertion:

The faculty and students of a professional school of social work should together be engaged in using the *great method of experimental research* [italics added] which we are just beginning to discover in our professional education programme, and which should be as closely knit into the work of a good school of social welfare as research has been embodied in the programme of a good medical school. (p. 55)

Traditionally, true experiments are seen as involving both pre- and posttests or posttests only. Because of the magical effects of randomization (given a sufficient sample size per each group of participants), one may usually safely infer that the groups are indeed equivalent on virtually any potential variable of interest, such as demographic characteristics like age, race, gender, marital status, as well as on measures of psychosocial functioning, health, and so forth. One may also assume that the groups were equivalent on what outcome measures were pertinent to the study before the members of each group received the experimental treatment or other control condition they were assigned to.

Perhaps the simplest true experiment can be diagramed as follows:

R   X   O
R   O

The R indicates that the groups were created using random assignment methods (such as by tossing a coin, using a table of random numbers, etc.), an approach that eliminates the possibility of bias creeping in and allowing certain people to have a greater or lesser likelihood of being assigned to a given condition. For example, if a social worker simply chooses participants to be assigned to one group or another, the more severely disabled clients, for example, might end up inadvertently being assigned to the no-treatment condition, thus setting up an apparent outcome favoring the treatment group. The X means, as usual, that some sort of experimental condition such as a novel treatment or intervention is being tested, and the O means a time when all participants are assessed using some reliable and valid outcome measure. If legitimate random assignment was used to create these two groups, they can be assumed to be similar before treatment, so any posttreatment differences on the outcome measures can be inferred to be the result of the top group's exposure to intervention X.

More than one treatment condition can be tested at the same time, as in this design:

$$
\begin{array}{ccc}
R & X & O \\
R & Y & O \\
R &   & O
\end{array}
$$

Here, two different treatments are being compared, both against each other, but also relative to no treatment. Further posttest assessments can be used to help determine the durability of any possible improvements, as in this:

$$
\begin{array}{cccc}
R & X & O & O \\
R & Y & O & O \\
R &   & O & O
\end{array}
$$

Here, as an example, the first observation may made immediately posttreatment and the second, say, six months later.

While posttest-only experiments are conducted, it is more common to incorporate formal pretests into such designs. This helps empirically establish the equivalence of your groups before intervention is given, which is a bit more solid an approach than assuming that randomization has exerted its leveling influence. Especially in studies with smallish groups (12 or 15 participants per condition) even with random assignment sometimes the vagaries of small numbers might result in nonequivalent groups. If you toss a coin enough times, you will eventually get a series of four heads or tails in a row. While this is unlikely (.5x.5x.5x.5=.06), given enough coin tosses, it will happen. Similarly, if you were tossing a coin to assign clients to a treatment or to a control condition, you might accidentally end up with two small groups unevenly distributed on some important variable, thus weakening your ability to make inferences about the effects of treatment. But, if you conduct formal pretests and empirically demonstrate that not only the groups are equivalent on demographic characteristics, but also in terms of their scores on relevant outcome measures, you are protected from such problems affecting your results.

Another advantage of pretests is that they permit the application of certain statistical tests such as an analysis of covariance, an approach that can help you take into account any differences that may exist on pretreatment measures when trying to determine if any posttreatment differences between groups are important.

Perhaps the simplest experimental design using a pretest can be diagramed as follows:

$$R \quad O \quad X \quad O$$
$$R \quad O \qquad O$$

Here you have two groups created using random assignment. Each group is pretested using some reliable and valid outcome measure: the top group then receives treatment, and both groups are assessed a second time. If the groups are equivalent at the pretest, and the treatment group is different (hopefully better!) at the posttest relative to the no-treatment group, then you have very strong grounds for concluding that treatment X caused these posttreatment differences.

Follow-up assessments can be added and additional control groups used as well to create a wide array of true experimental designs. See if you can understand what the following design depicts:

R	O	X	O	O	O
R	O	Y	O	O	O
R	O		O	O	O

If you concluded that it represents a randomized experimental design involving a pretest and posttreatment assessments on three separate occasions after treatment (for the two top groups) comparing the effects of interventions X and Y relative to each other and to no treatment, you would be on the right track. Let's see some real-life of examples of how social workers have used true experimental designs to evaluate psychosocial interventions practice.

Social work student Kelly Canady lived in Dublin, Georgia, a small town. A U.S. presidential election was coming up, and Kelly wanted to do something to help ensure that as many poor people voted as possible. Social workers have long been involved in get-out-and-vote campaigns. There are many ways to do this: flyers, public service announcements, voter registration campaigns, offering free rides to the polling station, and so forth. Kelly came up with something a bit different. He crafted a bipartisan letter stressing the importance of the election and of the need for everyone to vote, and he got the local chairs of the Republican and Democratic Party organizations in Dublin to sign it. He went to the voter registration office and obtained a printout of the names and addresses of all registered voters residing in the poorest section of Dublin, one containing numerous public housing projects and with over 90% African American residents. Such printouts are readily available to the public. There were about 4,000 voters on this list, and he randomly chose about 400 people for his project. These 400 voters were then randomly assigned to one of four conditions. The first group got no intervention at all. Those in the second group received by mail one of these reminder letters, scheduled so that it would arrive a couple of days before the election. The third group got two identical letters: one a week before the election and one a few days before. The fourth group got three identical letters, scheduled to arrive two weeks, one week, and a few days before the election.

After the election, Kelly went back to the voter registrar's office and found out whether his 400 voters actually voted in the recent election. This is public information—not who they voted for, but simply if they did indeed vote. He then tabulated the numbers and percentages of voters in each of his groups to see if those who got letters were more likely to vote than those who did not and if those who got two or three letters were more likely to vote that those who got only one. This design can be diagramed as follows:

$$
\begin{array}{ccc}
R & & O \\
R & X & O \\
R & Y & O \\
R & Z & O \\
\end{array}
$$

Here X means those folks who got one letter; Y those who got two; and Z those who got three. Would you like to know what Kelly found out regarding the effectiveness of these reminder letters in promoting voting among poor African Americans in Georgia? You will have to read Canady and Thyer (1990) to find out.

A very similar design was used by social worker Patrick Bordnick to evaluate the relative effectiveness of three different, active treatments for cocaine addiction relative to a placebo treatment. Participants were voluntary in-patients at a veterans' hospital located in Augusta, Georgia. This project's protocol was reviewed and approved by the university IRB, and all participants gave voluntary and informed consent. Treatment was pretty rigorous and consisted of three different forms of aversion therapy designed to reduce craving for cocaine. All the participants had had their lives seriously harmed by their cocaine addition and were really trying hard to overcome their drug use.

Patrick recruited 69 patients to participate in this study and, using random assignment methods, ended up with 20 assigned to the relaxation treatment condition; 17 to faradic (electric shock) aversion therapy; 16 to covert sensitization, a form of cognitively based aversion therapy; and 16 to emetic (using nausea-inducing drugs) aversion therapy. Note that, even using random assignment methods, Patrick ended up with four groups of uneven size. Aversion therapy involves pairing the ingestion of (fake) cocaine with the subsequent experience of an aversive stimulus (e.g., an uncomfortable electric shock, chemically-induced nausea or vomiting, or disgusting thoughts). Craving is considered to be an important variable in accounting for relapse among drug abusers, hence ways to reduce or eliminate craving are seen as important therapeutic venues.

In addition to this experimental protocol, all patients also received treatment as usual provided within the standard milieu of the hospital's 12-step-oriented drug abuse treatment program. Participants received about 12 sessions of the treatment they were assigned to, and the outcome measure consisted of their self-reports (systematized) of subjective craving for cocaine.

The design can be diagramed as follows:

R	W	O
R	X	O
R	Y	O
R	Z	O

In this design, W, X, Y, and Z refer to the four experimental conditions. It was found that the three aversion therapies reduced craving for cocaine, with emetic therapy proving to be the most effective in this regard. Patrick made the following conclusions:

> In summary, the aversion therapies investigated appear to provide initial evidence of their efficacy in reducing subjective craving in cocaine abusers. Replications need to be completed in order to increase the empirical validity and generalizability of these findings. (Bordnick, Elkins, Orr, Walters, & Thyer, 2004, p. 21).

The strength of Patrick's experimental design permitted the first conclusion, and the second recommendation is simply good, conservative practice given that this was the first experimental study of the role of these therapies in reducing cocaine craving. This was a pretty ambitious study, and one that was funded by the National Institute on Drug Abuse. It involved real clients with very serious problems. The ability to truly randomly assign participants to the various control groups is also another strength.

School social worker Rufus Larkin found himself in something of a pickle. He was receiving a large number of referrals from the teachers at the two elementary schools he worked at of kids who proved to be behaviorally disruptive in the classroom. The teachers wanted these kids to settle down, present fewer problems in class, and do better academically. Rufus could not see all the kids immediately, so he had to place some on a waiting list before he could assess and intervene. Rufus was also a doctoral student in social work at the University of Georgia and was faced with finding a dissertation topic. Hmmm. . . Could he deal with both situations at once? In conjunction with his major professor, Rufus proposed to evaluate the outcomes of the group therapy services he was providing to behaviorally disruptive elementary school kids and to take advantage of the naturally-occurring waiting list he developed to impose an experimental design in the provision of his services. He developed a fairly structured group-work protocol, involving eight sessions with specific activities and tasks associated with each session. His intervention was based on several structured cognitive-behavioral approaches to group therapy that had previously been shown to be effective with young people.

When a new kid was initially referred to him, he assessed the child on standardized measures of self-esteem, perceived self-control (both RAIs completed by the child), and separate "behavior grades" submitted by the teachers and teachers' aides, rated as D (worst behavior, scored as a 4), C, B, and A (best behavior, scored as a 1). Because he did not have the time or resources to see all the children at once, he used random assignment methods to designate some kids to enroll in group therapy immediately ($N=31$) and others later, creating a delayed treatment condition ($N=21$). His experimental design looked like this:

Immediate Treatment Group	R	O	X	O		O
Delayed Treatment Group	R	O		O	X	O

An analysis of the pretreatment demographic characteristics and outcome measures at the time of the first assessment found the two groups to be equivalent. Roughly speaking, the first group, those kids who got group therapy right away, got better immediately after social work intervention provided by Rufus (eight weeks of group therapy), and this group's gains were maintained at follow-up. However, the kids in the delayed treatment control condition did not improve at the time of their second assessment. Moreover, the differences between the two groups at the time of the second assessment were statistically significant, favoring the treated children. Fortunately, when the delayed treatment kids were later assessed after they received eight weeks of group therapy from Rufus, they too had markedly improved. Rufus's conclusions included the following:

> The results of this study are most encouraging, suggestive of the potential for early intervention with behaviorally disruptive youth. The protocol-based cognitive-behavioral group counseling was an inexpensive approach to service that was readily integrated into the school setting and well accepted by the teachers and administrators. The improvements we found can be attributed (by virtue of the experimental design) to the intervention itself, and not to the passage of time, to the assessment process, or to maturation effects. (Larkin & Thyer, 1999, p. 159)

Was this a perfect study? No, as described in the limitations discussed in the published paper. But it does represent a considerable improvement over quasi-experimental or preexperimental GRDs in terms of our ability to claim that treatment resulted in certain effects.

Lest the reader think that the potential for social workers to conduct true experiments is so limited to not be worth even considering, we urge you to consult a wonderful article by Sheldon Rose (1988) that appeared some years ago in the *Journal of Social Work Education*. Rose describes how he was routinely able to facilitate social workers designing and conducting true experiments on the outcomes of social work practice, and he makes reference to 18 such studies that he collaborated on. Social worker William Reid similarly worked with doctoral students who designed and published many examples of experimental designs used to evaluate the outcomes of the Task Centered Model of social work practice he developed (see Reid, 2000).

Many dozens of true experiments are now appearing each year within our social work literature, and many more appear in non-social work journals, all authored by professional social workers. An ever larger number of social workers are collaborating with authors within other disciplines in the design and conduct of experimental outcome studies of psychosocial interventions and, in some cases, biomedical treatments as well. For example, Gerald Hogarty, MSW, is the senior author on a number of articles evaluating treatment outcomes, that have appeared in the prestigious journal *Archives of General Psychiatry* (see, for example, Hogarty, Flesher, Ulrich, Carter, Greenwald, Pogue-Geile et al., 2004; Hogarty, McEvoy, Ulrich, Di-Barry, Bartone, Cooley, Hammill, et al., 1995; Hogarty & Ulrich, 1977). All told, Hogarty has authored over 50 articles appearing in mainstream psychiatric journals, most of which employed experimental designs over the past 30 years (see Thyer & Myers, 2006). There are an increasing number of social workers who have produced an impressive array of high-quality experimental outcome studies of the effects of psychosocial and biological treatments. These individuals include Gail Steketee, Robert Schilling, Steven P. Schinke, and Myrna Weissman. A quick look at any major database will disclose the productivity of these fine social work scholars. True experiments are a thriving element in the armamentarium of clinical and program evaluation methodologies.

HOW TO REPORT AND INTERPRET DATA*

Because almost all group outcome studies make use of some form of inferential (e.g., enabling you to draw conclusions about the reliability of any changes) statistics, you should either possess the skills yourself to design and conduct such inferential analyses (usually replying on some form of data-analysis software) or recruit a competent person to do this for you. Initially report on the characteristics of your various groups in terms of descriptive information and demographics, then include information about the outcome measures.

Describe the salient characteristics of the clients who actually participated in the study. If they were assigned to different conditions or if such conditions occurred naturally (e.g., clients who received immediate treatment versus those who were on a waiting list for a certain period, clients who received services from male social workers versus female social workers, etc.), describe the characteristics of each group separately. If you do this, there is no need to describe the features of all clients in the aggregate. At a minimum, include demographic factors such as age, rage, gender, ethnic background, and socioeconomic status if available. Report interval and ratio data in terms of Ns, means, and standard deviations, and categorical data in terms of frequencies and percentages. Never

---

*Portions of this section previously appeared in Thyer (2002a).

report a mean without its relevant N (number of people) and SD (standard deviation) or a percentage without the corresponding N.

Next, it is a good practice to restate your first hypothesis and then to report the data that directly address the corroboration or refutation of this particular hypothesis. If you have more than one outcome measure that tested this hypothesis, report the results for the first outcome measure in their entirety, then the results of the second outcome measure, and so on. Conclude with as clear a statement as is justifiable by your data regarding the support (or lack thereof) of this first hypothesis. Repeat this method of reporting for your second hypothesis, then your third, and so on. One important caveat: it is undesirable to break a clinical outcome study into smaller publishable reports with each being on a different outcome measure. This has been called "salami science," wherein anxious researchers try to author as many "least publishable units" as possible in order to build a résumé. Social workers should be aware that this practice is viewed with disfavor.

When you report the results of some statistically significant differences obtained using an inferential test, in addition to the name of the test (chi square, t-test, analysis of variance, etc.), the degrees of freedom, the actual test coefficient, and actual alpha level, you should always report some measure of effect size or proportion of variance potentially accounted for by the intervention(s). General guidance for doing this is contained in the *Publication Manual of the American Psychological Association* (American Psychological Association, 2001, pp. 25–26), and more specialized instructions can be found in various social work articles (e.g., Hudson, Thyer, & Stocks, 1985; Rubin & Conway, 1985; Stocks, 1987; Weinbach, 1989). This cautious practice is worthwhile since it curbs the perhaps natural tendency to ascribe undue importance to statistically reliable, but practically unimportant differences. This statistical conservatism is particularly worthwhile in clinical evaluation studies.

If you have completed a nomothetic study using one of the designs described in this chapter, you should know that no such study can ever be said to be truly finished until it has been written up in an understandable manner and published in some form that is readily accessible to the public. The most credible venue of publication is the scholarly article appearing in a quality peer-reviewed journal. Peer-reviewed journals use a certain system to screen and choose which articles to publish. When you submit your article to such a journal, the editor will assign several outside experts to review and critique your report, and this is usually done after the editor removes your name, affiliation, or other identification information from your manuscript. These "blind" reviewers critique your paper and make a recommendation to the editor to reject it, to accept it as is, or perhaps to ask you to revise it and only then to accept it. The editor digests these aggregate recommendations and makes a decision, informing you in due course. If it is eventually accepted, it will be printed (and increasingly available over the Internet via the journal's Web site). At that point, you can breath a sigh of relief and complete work on your next evaluation of practice.

5

Ethical Issues in the Design and Conduct of Evaluation Research

Adherence to both the letter and the spirit of our professional codes of ethics should permeate not only our direct practice activities, but also our efforts in the evaluation of practice outcomes. The *Code of Ethics* of the National Association of Social Workers (NASW, 1999) provides some guidance for us in this regard, and, while it is the most commonly cited ethical code for our professional, there are some others that are also credible. For example, the Clinical Social Work Federation, an independent membership association that many social workers belong to instead of or in addition to maintaining membership in the NASW, also has an extensive code of ethics that its members are obligated to adhere to (see http://www.cswf.org). Some social workers do not belong to any organization that is specifically for social workers, but instead choose to be active participants in some sort of specialty organization that reflects a practice modality. Examples include the American Association for Marriage and Family Therapy (http://www.aamft.org) or the Association for Behavior Analysis (http://www.abainternational.org), each of which has its own code of ethics. The book *Ethics for Behavior Analysts* by Jon Bailey and Mary Burch (2005) presents one set of ethical guidelines that the present authors are particularly impressed with, guidelines subscribed to by social workers and other professionals who are board-certified behavior analysts.

All these professional codes of ethics touch on the design and conduct of research, including evaluation of practice efforts. Such evaluation of practice efforts overlap considerably with the concept of practice itself, but, for the purposes of this volume, we will review the standards in the NASW *Code of Ethics*, which can be printed at no cost at from http://www.socialworkers.org.

WE HAVE AN OBLIGATION TO EVALUATE OUR OWN PRACTICE

It has long been recognized that evaluation of outcomes is an essential aspect of good practice, not only in social work, but in other human service fields. Here is what the NASW *Code of Ethics* (1999, sec. 5.02, p. 25) has to say on this issue:

> Social workers should monitor and evaluate policies, the imple-
> mentation of programs, and practice interventions. Social work-
> ers should promote and facilitate evaluation and research to con-
> tribute to the development of knowledge. Social workers should
> . . . fully use evaluation and research evidence in their professional
> practice.

And various standards produced by the NASW (1992) express similar senti-
ments:

> All school social work programs, new or long-standing, should
> be evaluated on an on-going basis to determine their relevance,
> effectiveness, efficiency, and contributions to the process of edu-
> cating children. (p. 16)

> Clinical social workers shall have . . . knowledge about and skills in
> using research to evaluate the effectiveness of a service. (NASW,
> 1989, p. 7)

Such views are not limited to social work. For example, professional counselors belonging to the American Counseling Association (1999) are enjoined through
their code of ethics that: "Counselors continually monitor their effectiveness as professionals and take steps to improve when necessary" (p. 6). And within the discipline of psychology:

> There are periodic, systematic, and effective evaluations of psycho-
> logical services. When the psychological service unit is a component
> of a larger organization, regular assessment of progress in achieving

goals is provided in the service delivery plan. Such evaluation could include consideration of the effectiveness of psychological services. (Board of Professional Affairs, 1987, p. 8)

Clearly, many different human service disciplines indicate that practitioners are expected to engage in clinical and program evaluation, and, therefore, your involvement in these activities is not only appropriate, but is also consistent with contemporary ethical standards.

ISSUES OF INFORMED CONSENT

Just as social workers are expected to obtain informed consent from clients prior to engaging them in assessment or treatment activities, obtaining informed consent is also indicated when one is undertaking evaluation activities with clients. Here is what the NASW *Code of Ethics* (1999, p. 25) says in this regard:

> (E) Social workers engaged in evaluation or research should obtain voluntary and written informed consent from participants, when appropriate, without any implied or actual deprivation of penalty for refusal to participate; without undue inducement to participate; and with due regard for participants' well-being, privacy, and dignity. Informed consent should include information about the nature, extent, and duration of the participation requested, and disclosure of the risks and benefits of participation in the research.

Now the qualifying phrase "when appropriate" in the above guideline leaves considerable room for ambiguity. Let us begin with some fairly clear situations. For example, if you wished to evaluate practice outcomes by asking clients to complete a RAI several times before, during, and after social work intervention, obtaining informed consent to do this could be imbedded in the general discussion of a treatment contract. This is the approach suggested by Bloom et al. (2006), who provide a model informed consent form, noting, "We again want to emphasize that *separate* consent for evaluation is not necessary since we view evaluation as just one component of overall practice. Thus, consent in this context is for practice to proceed and includes consent for evaluation" (p. 664, italics in original).

It is similarly clear that informed consent must be obtained prior to engaging clients in any type of nomothetic study that involves their assignment to different treatment conditions or exposure to an experimental (e.g., not commonly accepted or novel) treatment. Where there is ambiguity is a situation wherein you may wish to access existing client records containing measures of client functioning pre- and posttreatment and to analyze them within the context of a retrospectively created preexperimental pretest or posttest group design (O-X-O). The data may not have been gathered with the intention of being used in this manner, and the clients did not consent for such use. Moreover, the cases may have long since been closed or some clients may have moved away, died, or are otherwise inaccessible, rendering the retroactive gathering of informed consent impractical. Does the lack of informed consent forever preclude you from using existing client records in this manner? An extremely rigid and conservative interpretation of practice and research ethics may conclude precisely this. But, as a practical matter, most agency administrators usually permit such access, provided steps are taken to safeguard or delete personally identifiable information, and the use of such data is not usually seen as violating clients' rights or representing some other ethical lapse. Were this not the case, clinical outcomes research and other scientific investigations in many sensitive areas of practice (e.g., sex offenders, drug abusers, etc.) would be considerably limited if consent of the research participants were required.

INSTITUTIONAL REVIEW BOARD REVIEW AND APPROVAL

Almost all colleges and universities and many human service agencies (e.g., your state's Department of Children and Families, Department of Health, Department of Corrections, etc.) have an IRB whose mandate is to review and hopefully approve all research projects undertaken by employees of that university, college, or agency. Research has been defined at the federal level as systematic activities that are designed to test hypotheses, permit conclusions to be drawn, and contribute to knowledge that can be generalized.

Do your own efforts at evaluating the outcomes of social work practice meet this definition? Well, maybe. Certainly, if you are involved in a large-scale study that involves randomly assigning clients to an experimental treatment or to standard care with pre- and posttests, IRB review and approval obtained *before* you begin data collection are most certainly needed if you are employed in an agency that has an IRB. This would include all BSW, MSW, and PhD social work students completing a study as fulfillment of some academic degree requirement such as a thesis or dissertation. But what about the student in practicum who is asked by a supervisor or faculty liaison to undertake a single-system evaluation of his or her work with a single client? The information obtained will unlikely be generalizable in a scientific sense and will most likely be turned in, graded, and perhaps discarded as yet another hurdle in one's race to the social work degree. Most professionals agree that IRB review and approval is *not* necessary in such circumstances, particularly if one describes such activities as a responsible part of social work practice and not as research, then the IRB has no role. Calling such practices a quality assurance study, an evaluation of practice, an outcomes investigation, or a performance appraisal, are all phrases that can insulate you from the trip wire of using the word "research."

Having said that, it is important to emphasize that structured projects conveying more of a sense of systematic inquiry for research purposes such as a MSW thesis, a PhD dissertation, or even an independent study project used to fulfill some academic requirement should *always* be approved by the relevant IRB prior to beginning data collection. Any such project that uses human participants should follow this mandate, with exceptions being made for the comparatively rare study that does not involve the collection of data from human beings. Theoretical, historical, or methodological dissertations would be examples of projects for which IRB oversight is not needed.

An article by Cooksey (2005) bears on this discussion by posing the following question and answer:

> Q: I've heard that evaluation is not considered research and so is not subject to review. Is this true?
>
> A: It depends, and IRBs may not always agree with one another on when an evaluation project meets or does not meet the definition of research. A key issue in determining when an evaluation is considered research has to do with who will have access to the results

and in what form. For example, you might want to write about a project in a journal or a book. And you may be using the evaluation to contribute to knowledge about evaluation or about the substantive area of the evaluation. That likely makes your project research. If you are providing monitoring data to a manager, and the information will not be used by anyone outside of the agency or program, it might not be considered research. It is wise to have an IRB official or another qualified person who is not a part of the project help determine whether your evaluation is or is not research and to have documentation of that decision in writing. (p. 354)

Thus, one's intentions related to possibly publishing results (or even presenting them in another public forum such as a professional conference) represent a crucial factor in determining IRB oversight. If you intend to publish, IRB review is needed.

What happens when you begin a study without any intention to publish and without IRB approval, and, when it is concluded, you then realize that you have something that is really quite interesting and could be very publishable indeed? What are your options here? Not many. Conservative IRBs do not grant retrospective approval of any sort or under any circumstances, in which case you are stuck with a great project that you cannot publish. Others may be more open to an honest, pained explanation from you as you humbly request a retroactive blessing. But IRBs are often skeptical about such late requests as they have no way of knowing if you honestly did come to a belated realization that your project had publishable results or if you were trying the circumvent the need for prior approval, perhaps because of some time schedule you wanted to keep. A conservative practice would be to seek IRB approval if you foresee any possibility that you may wish to publish your results.

IRB review and approval are also not necessary when you are using publicly available information, even if it does contain personally identifiable information. Voter registration roles, a university's course evaluations on individual faculty, newspaper archives, and such can all be useful data sources for various research projects. One of the authors of this book recently undertook an examination of student course evaluations obtained from hundreds of social work classes taught over several years, dividing them by the type of instructor—regular faculty, community-based adjuncts, or PhD student instructors—to see if the instructional quality varies by the type of teacher. These course evaluations, broken down by class, semester taught, years, and individual faculty name are maintained on the university Web site from which they were downloaded. A Web site is a public venue, thus IRB review was not needed for this study.

IRB review is also not required when one is employed under the auspices of an agency that does not receive federal funding, such as a social worker in private practice or working for a private agency. However, should you wish IRB consultation, your local college or university IRB will usually be happy to assist you. A gray area would be if an employee of an agency that does have an IRB performs outside work as an independent or private consultant that is not a part of the employee's regular job assignment of responsibilities. An example would be a social work faculty member who is approached by a local faith-based social service agency (that does not receive any federal support) to undertake a program evaluation of the agency's services. So long as the faculty member does not use university resources (computers, software, phone, time, etc.) to engage in this project and undertakes it solely as a private consultant and not as a faculty member, then he or she would not be required (although it would most certainly be advisable) to seek university IRB approval to conduct this work. Here is how Cooksey (2005) addressed this issue:

> Q: I am an independent consultant. Do I need to have my work reviewed by an IRB? If so, where do I find one? I only hear about IRBs in connection with university research. Do I still have to get IRB approval?
>
> A: Whether you need IRB approval may depend on who is sponsoring the evaluation. If your work is supported by a federal agency. . . it requires IRB review if it is not exempt. The IRB in the federal agency or department might be willing to serve as the IRB of record in such a case or to facilitate your access to a board that would be willing to serve that purpose. (p. 357)

Clearly the issues surrounding the need for and obtaining IRB review and approval are complex, with many gray areas. However, take heart—when you get right down to it, the IRB application process is not necessarily onerous, although it may seem intimidating to the novice researcher. Prepare a few forms, a copy of your research protocol, assessment measures, and informed consent forms, all possibly submitted electronically, and your only additional requirement is to compose yourself with patience and await the board's decision. Whatever you do, do not put yourself or participate in any situation wherein IRB oversight was indicated, but not properly obtained prior to beginning data collection.

WHAT ABOUT PUBLISHING YOUR EVALUATION RESEARCH?

We believe that publishing the results of your evaluation efforts can be a tremendously rewarding undertaking. Both of the authors began their publishing careers with reporting narrative case histories describing innovative treatments provided to their clients (Myers, 1997; Thyer, 1981), and the personal and professional rewards involved in undertaking such work have been considerable. All the forms of evaluation research described in this book (SSDs and GRDs, preexperimental, quasi-experimental, and experimental), can find a ready home within the pages of the ever-expanding number of social work journals, which totaled over 70 in the English language according to one count (Thyer, 2005). A detailed description of the process of preparing and submitting a manuscript to a professional journal is beyond the scope of this volume, but we immodestly recommend *Successful Publishing in Scholarly Journals* (Thyer, 1994) as one very useful book that addresses this topic. The shorter article "How to Write Up a Social Work Outcome Study for Publication" (Thyer, 2002a) is another instructive resource. If you cannot track down a copy, write the author for a free reprint (Bthyer@mailer.fsu.edu).

The general idea, of course, is that the intellectual diversity of our disciplinary literature will be enhanced through an increasing proportion of social work practitioners, as well as academics, preparing and submitting outcome studies. Indeed, the NASW *Code of Ethics* (1999, p. 24, section 5.01, on the integrity of the profession) clearly states that "social workers should seek to contribute to the profession's literature and to share their knowledge at professional meetings and conferences" (sec. 5.0).

When you do disseminate your findings, the NASW *Code of Ethics* has something to say about that as well. The same section (5.01) advises that:

> (m) Social workers who report evaluation and research results should protect participant's confidentiality by omitting identifying information unless proper consent has been obtained authorizing disclosure. (p. 26)

> (n) Social workers should report evaluation and research findings accurately. They should not fabricate or falsify results and should take steps to correct any errors found in published data using standard publication methods. (p. 26)

By implication, paragraph m suggests that you do not need client consent to publish evaluation findings so long as personally identifying information is omitted, but this would be seen by some within the profession as a controversial position. We believe that the general field of evaluation research would quickly grind to a halt especially, in sensitive areas like domestic violence, child abuse and neglect, sexual offenses, and substance abuse, if professional social workers, physicians, psychologists, and others were required to obtain research participants' consent in order to publish the evaluation outcomes of their practice activities. We, of course, support the protection of client identities when preparing research reports, but we must be permitted to retain some "ownership" of the results of our own practice and evaluative endeavors. John Morgan said it very well as far back as 1949:

> I have spoken of the need for keeping records and statistics on the job as a necessary function of our professional job. I have an important footnote to that. We must not be so hypnotized by the need for professional confidentiality that we hide the results of our deeds from the penetrating mind of the research worker. (p. 152)

He also spoke respectfully of the contributions of small-scale evaluations in building a larger body of professional knowledge:

> A continuous succession of fruitful small research enterprises—putting all our weight behind inspiration wherever we find it—will do more for our cause that overelaboration in planning and frustration in performance. (p. 153)

WHO SHOULD COAUTHOR YOUR EVALUATION STUDIES WITH YOU?

Sometimes, practitioners and students who have engaged in the evaluation of practice and wish to write it up for some form of dissemination, such as a presentation at an in-service training, a grand rounds, a professional conference, or via a journal article, book chapter, or even in a book, are unsure who should be listed as a coauthor. Here is what the NASW *Code of Ethics* (1999) has to say on this topic:

> Section 4.08 Acknowledging Credit
> (A) Social workers should take responsibility and credit, including authorship credit, only for work they have actually performed and to which they have contributed.
>
> (B) Social workers should honestly acknowledge the work of and the contributions made by others. (p. 24)

The guidelines contained in the *Publication Manual of the American Psychological Association* (2001), standards followed by most social work journals, are even more explicit:

> Authorship is reserved for persons who receive primary credit and hold primary responsibility for a published work. Authorship encompasses, therefore, not only those who do the actual writing but also those who have made substantial scientific contributions to a study. Substantial scientific contributions may including formulating the problem or hypothesis, structuring the experimental design, organiz-

ing and conducting the statistical analysis, interpreting the results, or writing a major portion of the paper. Lesser contributions, which do not constitute authorship, may be acknowledged in a note. The general rule is that the principal contributor should appear first, with subsequent names in order of decreasing contribution. (pp. 350–351)

Sometimes, social workers may feel pressured or otherwise obliged to list clinical supervisors, academic advisors, or major professors as authors. In the absence of these individuals making a substantial contribution to the project, such courtesy authorships are strictly enjoined by the APA *Publication Manual*:

> Psychologists take responsibility and credit, including authorship credit, only for work they have actually performed or to which they have contributed. Mere possession of an institutional position, such as Department Chair, does not justify authorship credit. A student is usually listed as principal author on any multiple-authored article that is substantially based on the student's dissertation or thesis. (pp. 395–396)

Within the discipline of marriage and family therapy (which includes many social workers), Sections 6.2 and 6.3 of its code of ethics (see http://www.aamft.org) suggests similar standards:

> Marriage and family therapists assign publication credit to those who have contributed to a publication in proportion to their contributions and in accordance with customary professional publication standards. Marriage and family therapists do not accept or require authorship credit for a publication based on research from a student's program, unless the therapist made a substantial contribution beyond being a faculty advisor or research committee member. Coauthorship on a student thesis, dissertation or project should be determined in accordance with principles of fairness and justice.

Thus, any colleague, be it a social worker, psychologist, or marriage and family therapist, who pressures you to be granted authorship or who asserts senior authorship on a work he or she made a lesser contribution to is acting in an unethical and unprofessional manner. Such pressures should be resisted, perhaps by referring the colleague to the NASW or the Association of Marriage and Family Therapists (AAMFT) code of ethics or to the APA *Publication Manual*. Remember, it would also be deceptive on your part to collude in granting authorship of your work to an undeserving colleague. If the colleague is a member of the NASW, AAMFT, APA, or similar professional group, filing a formal ethics complaint with that organization is always an option.

KEEP AND SHARE YOUR DATA, AS RESPONSIBLY REQUESTED

One of the major principles of scientific inquiry, including the reporting of evaluation data, is that of transparency, reporting fully and accurately, warts and all, what you did and what you found. You may have primary data, not reported in published articles, that you should keep for several years after the dissemination of the results. There is no firm guideline on how long is long enough. Sometimes colleagues will be very interested in your work and will wish to examine your data in greater detail than permitted by the reports of summarized information in your paper or article, and it is not uncommon for an author of a research article to receive requests from others for copies of your primary data. This can be something as easy to provide as a statistical database or can involve requests more cumbersome to comply with, such as copies of actual surveys completed by clients, interview protocols, or RAIs. The general standard is to promptly provide the requested information for free or in return for a very nominal fee to cover the costs of copying and postage. The information provided should be purged of any personally identifying information related to your clients, of course, and you are under no obligation to provide it to unqualified individuals (e.g., a resident of a state mental hospital acting under some delusional system).

This ethic of transparency and sharing data promotes (in theory) further scientific advances. For example, Bruce was approached some years ago by Bill Nugent, a social work PhD student who had developed a new statistical technique and was in search of an appropriate set of data to apply this method to. His major professor, Walter Hudson, suggested that Bill approach Bruce to see if Bruce would provide his raw dissertation data to Bill. Bruce did, and Bill used it as the basis of testing his new method, a valuable study that not only was approved as Bill's PhD dissertation project, but also for an article he subsequently published in the top-quality journal, *Social Service Review*. This ethic of transparency and sharing also acts to inhibit fraud and deception in scientific research. There are occasional reports in the media of cases where published research is subsequently found out to have never been conducted at all or to have been based on altered or fabricated data. One of the best ways to uncover such instances is this practice of sharing data to qualified researchers.

6

Some Myths, Misconceptions, and Practical Considerations in Evaluation

There are a variety of reasons why social work practitioners do not attempt systematic evaluations of their own practice and programs. We have tried to address some of these in this book by claiming that such evaluations are part and parcel of ethical practice, providing information on locating and using useful outcome measures, and illustrating a wide array of research designs, including many that are relatively simple and easy to undertake. Our impression is that another significant reason such evaluations are relatively rare is the number of misconceptions about the evaluation research enterprise, myths and misconceptions that serve as intellectual barriers, deterring many in our profession from engaging in this fascinating area representing the intersection of research and practice. Some of these issues have been addressed in prior publications (Thyer, 1991, 1992, 2002a, 2002b) or in chapters in books that may not be readily accessible to you, so we would like to reiterate and expand upon these issues in this book focused on North American social workers.

MYTH NUMBER 1: THE MAJOR PURPOSE OF RESEARCH IS TO DEVELOP AND TEST THEORY

Traditional social and behavioral science has long stressed that the purpose of research is to contribute to the development of formal theory. This emphasis is so pervasive that many sources claim that any study that does not contribute to theory can be seen as second-rate or as unscientific. One edition of a widely used social work research textbook exemplifies this attitude:

> Some studies make no use of theory at all. Of course, conducting such atheoretical studies that have little or no relevance out-

side their pragmatic purposes for a particular agency does little to build social work knowledge. Consequently, some do not call such studies "scientific research," preferring instead to label them as administrative data-gathering. (Rubin & Babbie, 1997, p. 55)

We find this dismissive attitude toward pragmatic efforts in evaluating one's own practice or agency's programs to be both puzzling and injurious to the practice evaluation movement so stressed by other voices within our field. The reality is that many social work programs and interventions are *not based* on some clearly explicated social or behavioral science theory, and practitioners' awareness of this may lead them to believe that studies on the effectiveness of such atheoretical programs are not worth it. Try the following experiment: ask some social work practitioners you know to describe the formal behavioral science theory their program or interventions are based on. In many, but certainly not all instances, you will be met with a puzzled look, a shrug, or an "I don't know." Is your state's child protective services program based on any formal theory on the etiology of child abuse or does it have a well-developed theory for how its interventions work? Probably not.

Now certainly there are many instances wherein psychosocial interventions are based on theory. For example, Alcoholics Anonymous is based on the biological theory that uncontrolled drinking is the result of an allergic reaction to alcohol. Contingency management approaches to treating substance abusers or the chronically mentally ill are based on operant theory and multisystemic therapy, widely used among juvenile delinquents, is largely derived from social learning theory. We believe and have contended elsewhere that although many social work programs are based on one or more formal theories, many are not, but it is possible and desirable to undertake systematic evaluations of the effectiveness of all such services, regardless of their apparent theoretical foundations or lack thereof (see Thyer, 1994, 2001, 2002c).

The late Harold Lewis (1965) alluded to the negative consequences of this myth over 40 years ago:

Some would reject agency-based research as inconsequential because it is directed to immediate practice ends rather than development of theory. Others deny the value of agency-based research in helping to clarify and add to significant problems encountered in day-to-day practice. Both represent attitudes that can, and often do, prove the most costly of all causes of "waste" in the utilization of the efforts of the research worker. (p. 24)

So, if you find yourself in the position of practicing within a program that lacks a theoretical foundation and cannot see any possible contributions toward the development of behavioral science theory through conducting an evaluation of your practice, do not let this deter you from moving ahead. There is a strong segment within our profession calling for such evaluations, even of programs not clearly based on a theory.

MYTH NUMBER 2: EVALUATION RESEARCH MUST USE SAMPLES OF CLIENTS RANDOMLY SELECTED FROM A LARGER POPULATION OF INTEREST

This myth stems from the idea that research knowledge must be "generalizable," in other words, to contribute to knowledge and theory. However, program evaluation, on the other hand, is not particularly concerned with developing generalizable knowledge so much as it is to answer particular questions whose answers are important to service providers, administrators, and funding sources.

Almost all evaluation research is usually aimed at evaluating local programs and makes use, therefore, of samples of convenience or availability. The myth that your potential study clients must be somehow representative of the larger population of clients with similar problems tends to discourage social workers from undertaking evaluation studies. The generalizability of a finding obtained from a convenience sample (which encompasses most such inquiries) may be established via the process of replication, having other outcome studies address the same intervention as applied to another group of clients with the same problem, and (hopefully) obtaining a similar result. We certainly agree that it is desirable to use a sample of clients who are representative of the entire population of people with a given problem, but this is almost never possible. So go ahead and evaluate using your clients.

MYTH NUMBER 3: EVALUATION RESEARCH RELATED TO A PARTICULAR PSYCHOSOCIAL PROGRAM MUST BE BASED ON A CLEAR UNDERSTANDING OF THE CAUSES OF THE PROBLEM

How many client problems addressed by social workers have a clearly established etiology? Homelessness? Domestic violence? Child abuse and neglect? Racial discrimination? No. Nope. Nada. Nyet. The unpleasant reality is that the issues practitioners in our field deal with are so incredibly complex and multiply determined that clear and empirically supported conceptualizations of the true causes of these problems continue to elude us in almost every case. Yet, the idea, perhaps a lingering influence of the social survey movement of the last century, that we need to have a complete descriptive and causal understanding of problems before we can intervene, remains a pervasive one. If you accept this idea, a myth in our opinion, then you will likely be immobilized, deterred from thinking you can evaluate the outcomes of your own program or practices.

Our lack of etiological understanding of the causes of complex social problems does not prevent us from trying to intervene nor should it inhibit our efforts to evaluate the outcomes of these programs. Take something "simple," like high school dropout. Frankly, it was easier to get a human being to the moon and safely back than it has been for us to figure out the causes of kids dropping out of school. Regardless, high school dropout prevention programs are widespread. Millions of taxpayers' dollars are being expended in such efforts, all without clearly knowing why adolescents drop out. Our view is that if a program is worth undertaking, it is also worth evaluating!

MYTH NUMBER 4: EVALUATION RESEARCH MUST DETERMINE HOW AN INTERVENTION WORKS

While it is certainly nice to know with some certainty how an intervention works, lack of this knowledge does not prevent us from finding out the impact of interventions. As a simple example, we do not have a really clear understanding of how aspirin alleviates headache pain or how the newest antipsychotic drug works. But this lack of knowledge about these interventions' mechanisms of action does not prevent researchers from undertaking systematic evaluations of their effects, good and bad.

The preschool program called Head Start seems to be one intervention that is helpful in preparing youngsters for school, and, even though its positive benefits seem to have been well established, exactly how Head Start works remains unclear.

Michael Scriven is a past president of the American Evaluation Association, and he has distinguished three types of evaluation: those he calls a Black Box evaluation, wherein the evaluator has little idea how the intervention works; Gray Box evaluation, wherein research provides some indications on how an intervention works; and Clear Box evaluation, wherein the mechanisms responsible for an intervention's effectiveness are compellingly established (Scriven, 1999). It may not be a good idea to undertake a Clear Box study until several Black Box evaluations have shown that you have something worth investigating. In fact, we know of no examples of a Clear Box evaluation of a social work intervention. But the myth that you need to understand how your intervention works in order to conduct a useful evaluation of that service may deter social workers from undertaking such studies. This is unfortunate since simply determining that clients have (or have not) gotten better is a very useful undertaking, even if you cannot determine the inner workings or causal mechanisms of why they got better.

MYTH NUMBER 5: YOU CAN ONLY DO EVALUATION RESEARCH ON EXTREMELY WELL PROCEDURALIZED INTERVENTIONS

Clear specification of the "independent variable" (treatment) is indeed characteristic of conventional behavioral science, but social work practice as an independent variable largely lacks this degree of precision. Child protective services, school social work, and community organizing are all difficult to proceduralize. If one accepts the myth that your treatment must be well proceduralized in order to evaluate it, then you will naturally be discouraged from undertaking such appraisals of the outcomes of practice. We social workers are different from conventional social and behavioral scientists in that our independent variables are not always well described. Sometimes they are, of course. Social worker Craig LeCroy (1994) has assembled a very useful set of treatment manuals for practice with children and adolescents related to common issues such as eating disorders, social skills training, drug abuse, and depression. Social worker Myrna Weissman has pioneered the development of treatment manuals for interpersonal psychotherapy, and our own discipline's Gail Steketee has done the same for therapy with persons meeting the criteria for obsessive-compulsive disorder. Social work faculty member Mary Ann Test has helped develop and test a psychoeducation program called Assertive Community Treatment, aimed at enhancing the community functioning of individuals with chronic mental illness. So it is not impossible to develop clear protocols and treatment manuals for social services, and it certainly facilitates both their initial testing and replication of findings. But it is not an essential requirement.

MYTH NUMBER 6: THE FIRST STEP IN EVALUATION RESEARCH IS TO CREATE YOUR OUTCOME MEASURE(S)

The novice program evaluator is often tempted to develop a new scale, RAI, or survey to assess the success of his or her program. Avoid this temptation like the plague. The design and validation of a scale or survey is a major project in and of itself, and a program evaluation is no place to try to develop such a measure. If you ignore this advice and prepare and use your own scale, your entire study's results may be called into question because the reader will have no evidence that your new measure is a reliable and valid one. This will also reduce the chances that you will be able to publish your findings in a reputable journal since having a credible outcome measure is pretty much a requirement for such studies to be published. Instead, select from the plethora of already existing and previously published outcome measures as described in chapter 2, and use these. If you do decide to develop your own measure complete this undertaking first, and only use it in your evaluation work after it has been demonstrated to be reliable and valid.

MYTH NUMBER 7: YOU MUST CONTROL FOR MOST RELEVANT THREATS TO INTERNAL VALIDITY

This myth is based on the conceptual confusion between studies that aim simply to see if change occurred versus studies that try to prove a causal link between treatment and outcome. If you have a simple question such as, "Did Ms. Lopez's depression improve over the course of social work treatment?" then a simple A-B SSD is sufficient to answer that question. If your question is more ambitious, as in, "Did social work treatment cause Ms. Lopez's depression to improve?" then a much stronger design is called for, such as one involving withdrawal phases or an MBL design. Or, in the nomothetic research tradition, if your question is, "Was the recidivism rate one year after referral to a drug court less than 10% for the 76 adolescents seen at the drug court during 2006?" this, too, can be satisfactorily answered using a simple design like the X-O pretest-posttest design. Strong controls to enhance internal validity are not needed since the claims being made are simple ones and not causal.

The fact is that the agency contexts wherein most social work interventions take place do not permit the degree of experimental control over clients' lives to allow the use of rigorous experimental designs. We cannot usually randomly assign clients to a no-treatment condition or to a placebo-treatment group, and sometimes pretests are not possible. So the solution is to do the best you can, realizing that it is better to have credible answers to simple questions compared to no answers to any questions. And realize that small-scale, uncontrolled evaluations are published all the time in some very good journals.

MYTH NUMBER 8: YOU MUST RANDOMLY ASSIGN CLIENTS TO VARIOUS CONTROL AND EXPERIMENTAL GROUPS

See the response to Myth Number Seven. Random assignment is a feature of only some types of experimental designs and are not needed at all for preexperimental and quasi-experimental studies. Your inability to randomly assign clients need not deter you from evaluating your own practice. Instead, use a more flexible design that does not have this requirement.

MYTH NUMBER 9: YOU MUST DETERMINE THE SAMPLE SIZE OF YOUR GROUPS BEFORE STARTING YOUR EVALUATION

While this feature may be desirable in some types of behavioral science research, you cannot always accurately predict how many clients will seek services during your evaluation study's time frame. In evaluation research, you must often accept whatever sample size you can practically obtain. Social work evaluators study clients in need, not an endless supply of undergraduates enrolled in psychology classes. Our research must make use of available clients.

MYTH NUMBER 10: YOU MUST OBTAIN FORMAL INFORMED CONSENT FROM YOUR CLIENTS TO EVALUATE OUTCOMES

This depends, as discussed in the prior chapter. If you are evaluating an experimental intervention or wish to randomly assign clients to different conditions, then informed consent may well be an ethical responsibility. But if you are making use of data found in existing agency records or evaluating the outcomes of treatment as is usually provided with no extra demands made upon clients or risks imposed upon them, then informed consent may not be essential. Such evaluation efforts can be seen as simply a component of ethical, professional practice, providing of course that you appropriately disguise personally identifying information about the clientele in your reports.

The NASW's *Code of Ethics* (1999) has this to say on the topic:

> Social workers engaged in evaluation of research should obtain voluntary and written informed consent from participants, *when appropriate* [italics added], without any or actual deprivation or penalty for refusal to participate. (p. 25)

It is difficult to see how working with clients in evaluating the outcomes of routine services provided to them could be construed as "research." It is much more aligned with good practice, which, of course, usually requires a clear oral or written treatment contract, and this would appear to comply with the above standard.

MYTH NUMBER 11: YOU MUST MASTER AND MAKE USE OF COMPLEX INFERENTIAL STATISTICS

Many social workers are intimidated by studying statistics; in fact, many MSW programs do not require that students complete a single graduate course in statistics. Thus, if a social worker is not very knowledgeable about them and accepts this myth, she or he may be deterred from attempting evaluation studies. The reality is that many evaluation designs, including most SSDs and some group studies, make use of very simple statistics or even none at all. If, however, your design does necessitate the use of statistical techniques beyond your abilities, all is not lost. You could, perhaps, try to learn these methods on your own. That is always a good idea. But if you choose not to do this, you can usually find a helpful colleague within your agency or at a nearby agency to assist you. Your colleague may do this as a favor or you may pay the person. In some cases, he or she will be glad to lend assistance in return for a coauthorship on any paper or publication that emerges from the project. This is entirely legitimate and ethical. But it is always best to seek out such statistical consultation *before* you begin your study.

MYTH NUMBER 12: SINCE ABSOLUTELY CERTAIN KNOWLEDGE IS NOT POSSIBLE IN SOCIAL SCIENCE, ATTEMPTING EVALUATION STUDIES IS NOT WORTHWHILE

This myth overlooks the importance of taking small steps toward a goal and of achieving approximations to nature's truths. Science has always recognized that its findings are provisional, capable of being amended or refuted as new data are gathered. None of the studies the authors have published can be considered to be perfect exemplars of research, but all of them have been subjected to blind review, critically analyzed, and ultimately recommended for publication. This myth is based upon a misconception of what science claims, a view that does not claim that certain knowledge is always obtainable in real-life settings—only in principle that it is possible. Is the space program of the United States perfect? By no means. Are our public health efforts free from any mistakes? Indeed not. We should not, therefore, expect perfection or certainty from social work practice and research.

The eminent social work scholar Aaron Rosen (1983) addressed this myth as follows:

> It is important that practitioners be taught to appreciate the incremental nature of knowledge gained through scientific research. Viewing the products of research in terms of uncertainty reduction rather than instilling expectations for absolute knowledge should render practitioners more tolerant of the uncertainty still remaining in phenomena under investigation. Thus reduction in uncertainty gained through research should not be compared with an ideal but unlikely state of absolute knowledge, but with an absolute state of ignorance regarding the phenomena. (p. 11)

This myth is also refuted by the obvious stress placed upon the self-evaluation of social work practice found in the curriculum standards of the Council on Social Work Education and in the ethical and practice guidelines established by the NASW.

CONCLUDING REMARKS

We hope that our overview of some methods that can be used by social work practitioners to evaluate the results of their own practice has persuaded you that such efforts can be a practical and rewarding undertaking. We have found, along with so many others in our field, that our clinical work and educational endeavors provide us with fertile soil to plant the seeds of simple GRDs or SSDs. Although we are currently social work academics, we began our professional careers as service providers in direct practice settings and retain our profound respect for the valuable role social work students and practitioners can play in the conceptualization, design, conduct, and reporting of evaluation studies. We have illustrated this book with actual examples from our own efforts in this regard, many of which were small scale and possessed significant flaws. But this reflects the realities of evaluation research. The perfect study has yet to be published. And, by illustrating how some less-than-perfect examples of intervention research have been published, we hope that we have encouraged you to think more seriously about undertaking similar studies of your own.

Outcomes research in social work has made remarkable advances over the past few decades. Randomized controlled clinical trials are now routinely published in our professional journals, and even meta-analyses of the effects of social work intervention are not uncommon. The number of our disciplinary journals has exploded, including a significant addition of new research journals. But there is a serious need for social work *practitioners* to be more involved in evaluation studies. We will close with a quotation from John Morgan (1949):

> I have already made much of the need for lay partnership in our research work. Only by using it will our researches be more than Dead Sea fruit. Only when all who are engaged in social work look forward with eagerness for the results of good research to improve their practice will research findings be used. The central pillar of

our framework . . . is a profession in which every worker acknowledges some responsibility for research, on the job, in the office, in the classroom, in committee, and on the board. These contributions will vary with their talents but all must have the essential—a questing mind. (p. 154)

References

Abbott, E. (1931). *Social welfare and professional education.* Chicago: University of Chicago Press.

Aeby, V. G., Manning, B., Thyer, B. A., & Carpenter-Aeby, T. (1999). Comparing outcomes of an alternative school offered with and without intensive family involvement. *The School Community Journal, 9,* 17–32.

American Counseling Association. (1999). *Code of ethics.* Alexandria, VA: Author. Retrieved October 12, 2006, from http://www.counseling.org/Resources/CodeOfEthics/TP/Home/CT2.aspx

American Psychiatric Association. (2000). *Diagnostic and statistical manual of mental disorders* (4th ed., text revision). Washington, DC: Author.

American Psychological Association. (2001). *Publication manual of the American Psychological Association* (5th ed.). Washington, DC: Author.

Angell, R. C. (1954). A research basis for welfare practice. *Social Work Journal, 35,* 145–148.

Baer, D. M., Harrison, R., Fradenburg, L., Petersen, D., & Milla, S. (2005). Some pragmatics in the valid and reliable recording of directly observed behavior. *Research on Social Work Practice, 15,* 440–451.

Bailey, J. S., & Burch, M. R. (2005). *Ethics for behavior analysts.* Mahwah, NJ: Erlbaum.

Baker, L., & Thyer, B. A. (1999). Family social work intervention to increase parental compliance with infant apnea monitor use in the home. *Journal of Family Social Work, 3*(3), 21–27.

Baker, L., & Thyer, B. A. (2000). Promoting parental compliance with home infant apnea monitor use. *Behaviour Research and Therapy, 38,* 285–296.

Barker, K. L., & Thyer, B. A. (2000). Differential reinforcement of other behavior in the treatment of inappropriate behavior and aggression in an adult with mental retardation at a vocational center. *Scandinavian Journal of Behaviour Therapy, 29*, 37–42.

Barker, R. L. (Ed.). (2003). *The social work dictionary* (5th ed.). Washington, DC: NASW Press.

Blackman, D. K., Gehle, C., & Pinkston, E. M. (1979). Modifying eating habits of the institutionalized elderly. *Social Work Research and Abstracts, 15*, 18–24.

Blenkner, M., Bloom, M., & Nielsen, M. (1971). A research and demonstration project of protective services. *Social Casework, 52*, 489–506.

Bloom, M., Fischer, J., & Orme, J. (2006). *Evaluating practice: Guidelines for the accountable professional* (5th ed.). Boston: Allyn & Bacon.

Board of Professional Affairs. (1987). General guidelines for providers of psychological services. *American Psychologist, 42*, 1–12.

Bordnick, P. S., Elkins, R. L., Orr, T. E., Walters, P., & Thyer, B. A. (2004). Evaluating the relative effectiveness of three aversion therapies designed to reduce craving among cocaine abusers. *Behavioral Interventions, 19*, 1–24.

Bruno, F. (1936). *The theory of social work*. New York: D.C. Health.

Buchanan, J. P., Dixon, D. R., & Thyer, B. A. (1997). A preliminary evaluation of treatment outcomes at a veterans' hospital's inpatient psychiatry unit. *Journal of Clinical Psychology, 53*, 853–858.

Butterfield, W. H., & Parson, R. (1973). Modeling and shaping by parents to develop chewing behavior in their mentally retarded child. *Journal of Behavior Therapy and Experimental Psychiatry, 4*, 285–287.

Canady, K., & Thyer, B. A. (1990). Promoting voting behavior among low income black voters: An experimental investigation. *Journal of Sociology and Social Welfare, 17*(4), 109–116.

Capp, H., Thyer, B. A., & Bordnick, P. S. (1997). Evaluating improvement over the course of adult psychiatric hospitalization. *Social Work in Health Care, 25*, 55–66.

Carr, J. E., & Burkholder, E. O. (1998). Creating single-subject design graphs with Microsoft Excel. *Journal of Applied Behavior Analysis, 31*, 245–251.

Carrillo, D. F., Gallant, J. P., & Thyer, B. A. (1993). Training MSW students in interviewing skills: An empirical evaluation. *Arete, 18*(1), 12–19.

Carrillo, D. F., & Thyer, B. A. (1994). Advanced standing and two-year program MSW students: An empirical investigation of foundation interviewing skills. *Journal of Social Work Education, 30,* 278–288.

Claghorn, K. H. (1908). The use and misuse of statistics in social work. In A. Johnson (Ed.), *Proceedings of the National Conferences on Charities and Corrections* (pp. 234–251). Fort Wayne, IN: National Conference on Charities and Corrections.

Clement, J. A., & Greene, G. J. (2002). Assessment and treatment for persons with bipolar disorder. In A. R. Roberts & G. Greene (Eds.), *Social workers' desk reference* (pp. 575–581). New York: Oxford University Press.

Conboy, A., Auerbach, C., Beckerman, A., Schnall, D., & LaPorte, H. H. (2000). MSW student satisfaction with using single-system design computer software to evaluate social work practice. *Research on Social Work Practice, 10,* 127–138.

Cooksey, L. J. (2005). The complexity of the IRB process: Some of the things you wanted to know about IRBs but were afraid to ask. *American Journal of Evaluation, 26,* 353–361.

Fischer, J., & Corcoran, K. (2007). *Measures for clinical practice: A sourcebook* (4th ed.). New York: Free Press.

Corsini, R. (2002). *The dictionary of psychology.* New York: Brunner-Routledge.

Crolley, J., Roys, D., Thyer, B. A., & Bordnick, P. S. (1998). Evaluating outpatient behavior therapy of sex offenders: A pretest-posttest study. *Behavior Modification, 22,* 485–501.

Curtis, G. C., & Thyer, B. A. (1983). Fainting on exposure to phobic stimuli. *American Journal of Psychiatry, 140,* 771–774.

Ell, K. (1996). Social work research and healthcare practice and policy: A psychosocial research agenda. *Social Work, 41,* 583–592.

Faul, A., & Hudson, W. W. (1997). The Index of Drug Involvement: A partial validation. *Social Work, 42,* 565–572.

Fischer, J. (Ed.). (1976). *The effectiveness of social casework.* Springfield, IL: Charles C Thomas.

Fisher, W. W., Kelley, M. D., & Lomas, J. E. (2003). Visual aids and structured criteria for improving visual inspection and interpretation of single-case designs. *Journal of Applied Behavior Analysis, 36,* 387–406.

Gary-McCormick, E., Thyer, B. A., Panton, T. M., & Myers, L. L. (2000). The association be-tween appointment-keeping and birth outcome in a prenatal care program for high-risk women. *Journal of Family Social Work, 4*(1), 47–58.

Gerardot, R. J., Thyer, B. A., Mabe, P. A., & Posten, P. M. (1992). The effects of psychiatric hospitalization on behaviorally disordered children: A preliminary evaluation. *The Psy-chiatric Hospital, 23,* 65–68.

Glueck, E. T. (1936). *Evaluative research in social work.* New York: Columbia University Press.

Gordon, L. B. (1980). Preferential drug abuse: Defenses and behavioral correlates. *Journal of Personality Assessment, 44,* 345–350.

Green, G., & Shane, H. C. (1994). Science, reason, and facilitated communication. *Journal of the Association for Persons With Severe Handicaps, 19,* 151–172.

Greenwood, E. (1957). Social work research: A decade of reappraisal. *Social Service Review, 31,* 311–320.

Gregory, R. L. (Ed.). (1987). *The Oxford companion to the mind.* New York: Oxford University Press.

Grehan, P., & Moran, D. J. (2005). Constructing single-subject reversal design graphs using Microsoft Word: A comprehensive tutorial. *The Behavior Analyst Today, 6,* 235–242.

Hamilton, G. (1940). *Theory and practice in social casework.* New York: Columbia University Press.

Hawkins, R. P., & Mathews, J. R. (1999). Frequent monitoring of clinical outcomes: Research and accountability for clinical practice. *Education and Treatment of Children, 22,* 177–135.

Heckman, A. A., & Stone, A. (1947, October). Testing casework results: Forging new tools. *Survey Mid-Monthly, 83,* 267–270.

Hogarty, G. E., McEvoy, J. P., Ulrich, R. F., DiBarry, A. D., Bartone, P., Cooley, S., Hammill, K., Carter, M., Munetz, M. R., & Perel, J. (1995). Pharmacotherapy of impaired affect in recovering schizophrenic patients. *Archives of General Psychiatry, 52,* 29.

Hogarty, G. E., Flesher, S., Ulrich, R., Carter, M., Greenwald, D., Pogue-Geile, M., Kechavan, M., Cooley, S., DeBarry, A. L., Garrett, A., Parepally, H., & Zoretich, R. (2004). Cogni-tive enhancement therapy for schizophrenia: Effects of a two-year randomized trial on cognition and memory. *Archives of General Psychiatry, 61,* 866–876.

Hogarty, G. E., & Ulrich, R. F. (1977). Temporal effects of drug and placebo in delaying relapse in schizophrenic outpatients. *Archives of General Psychiatry, 34,* 297–301.

Hsieh, D. K., & Kirk, S. A. (Eds.) (2005). The limits of diagnostic criteria: The role of social context in clinicians' judgments of mental disorder. In S. A. Kirk (Ed.), *Mental disorders in the social environment: Critical perspectives* (pp. 45–61). New York: Columbia University Press.

Hudson, W. W., & McIntosh, S. R. (1981). The assessment of spouse abuse: Two quantifiable dimensions. *Journal of Marriage and the Family, 43,* 873–886.

Hudson, W. W., & Thyer, B. A. (1987). Research measures and indices in direct practice. In A. Minahan (Ed.), *Encyclopedia of social work* (Vol. 2, pp. 487–498). Silver Spring, MD: NASW Press.

Hudson W. W., Thyer, B. A., & Stocks, J. T. (1985). Assessing the importance of experimental outcomes. *Journal of Social Service Research, 8,* 87–98.

Hunt, J. M., & Kogan, L. S. (1952). *Measuring results in social casework: A manual on judging movement.* New York: Family Service Association of America.

Jacobson, J. W., Foxx, R. M., & Mulick, J. A. (Eds.). (2005). *Controversial therapies for developmental disabilities: Fad, fashion and science in professional practice.* Mahwah, NJ: Erlbaum.

Jordan, C., & Franklin, C. (Eds.). (2003). *Clinical assessment for social workers: Quantitative and qualitative approaches* (2nd ed.). Chicago: Lyceum Press.

Kazi, M. A. F. (1998). *Single-case evaluation by social workers.* Brookfield, VT: Ashgate.

Kazi, M. A. F., Mantysaari, M., & Rostila, I. (1997). Promoting the use of single-case designs: Social work experiences from England and Finland. *Research on Social Work Practice, 7,* 311–328.

Kazi, M. A. F., & Wilson, J. (1996). Applying single-case evaluation in social work. *British Journal of Social Work, 26,* 699–717.

Larkin, R., & Thyer, B. A. (1999). Evaluating cognitive-behavioral group counseling to improve elementary school students' self-esteem, self-control, and classroom behavior. *Behavioral Interventions, 14,* 147–161.

Lawrence, S. A., Wodarski, J. S., & Wodarski, J. (2002). Behavioral medicine paradigm: Behavioral interventions for chronic pain and headache. *Journal of Human Behavior in the Social Environment, 5*(2), 1–14.

LeCroy, C. W. (1994). *Handbook of child and adolescent treatment manuals.* New York: Lexington Books.

Levine, R. R. (2002). Glossary. In A. R. Roberts & G. J. Greene (Eds.), *Social workers' desk reference* (pp. 829–849). New York: Oxford University Press.

Lewis, H. (1965). The use and place of research in the administration of the social agency. *Child Welfare, 44,* 21–25.

Ligon, J., & Thyer, B. A. (2000a). Client and family satisfaction with brief community mental health, substance abuse, and mobile crisis services in an urban setting. *Crisis Intervention, 6,* 93–99.

Ligon, J., & Thyer, B. A. (2000b). Community inpatient crisis stabilization in an urban setting: Evaluation of changes in psychiatric symptoms. *Crisis Intervention, 5,* 163–169.

Lilienfeld, S. O., Lynn, S. J., & Lohr, J. M. (Eds.). (2003). *Science and pseudoscience in clinical psychology.* New York: Guilford.

MacDonald, M. E. (1952). Some essentials in the evaluation of social casework. *Journal of Psychiatric Social Work, 22*(3), 135–137.

Maeser, N., & Thyer, B. A. (1990). Teaching boys with severe mental retardation to serve themselves during family-style meals. *Behavioural Residential Treatment, 5,* 239–246.

Mattaini, M. A. (1993). *More than a thousand words: Graphs for clinical practice.* Washington, DC: NASW Press.

Maxwell, J. P. (2003). The imprint of childhood physical and emotional abuse: A case study on the use of EMDR to address anxiety and a lack of self-esteem. *Journal of Family Violence, 18,* 281–286.

Meyer, C. H. (1973). Practice models—The new ideology? *Smith College Studies in Social Work, 43,* 85–107.

Meyer, H. J., & Borgatta, E. F. (1959). *An experiment in mental patient rehabilitation.* New York: Russell Sage Foundation.

Miller, L. K., & Miller, O. L. (1970). Reinforcing self-help group activities of welfare recipients. *Journal of Applied Behavior Analysis, 3,* 57–64.

Moore, L. S., Dettlaff. A. L., & Dietz, T. J. (2004). Using the Myers-Briggs Type Indicator in field instruction supervision. *Journal of Social Work Education, 40,* 337–349.

Moran, D. J., & Hirschbine, B. (2002). Constructing single-subject reversal design graphs using Microsoft Excel: A comprehensive tutorial. *The Behavior Analyst Today, 3,* 180–188.

Morgan, J. S. (1949). Research in social work: A frame of reference. *Social Work Journal, 30,* 148–154.

Mosier, C. I. (1947). A critical examination of the concepts of face validity. *Educational and Psychological Measurement, 7,* 191–205.

Mosley, D., Thyer, B. A., & Larrison, C. (2001). Development and preliminary findings of the Mosley Forensic Competency Scale. *Journal of Human Behavior in the Social Environment, 4*(1), 41–48.

Mullen, E. (1995). A review of Research Utilization in the Human Services. *Social Work, 40,* 282–283.

Mullen, E., & Magnabosco, J. (1997a). Concluding comments. In E. J. Mullen & J. Magnabosco (Eds.), *Outcomes measurement in the human services* (pp. 308–320). Washington, DC: NASW Press.

Mullen, E. J., & Magnabosco, J. (Eds.). (1997b). *Outcomes measurement in the human services.* Washington, DC: NASW Press.

Myers, L. L. (1997). Exposure therapy in the brief treatment of an elevator phobia. *Scandinavian Journal of Behaviour Therapy, 26,* 22–26.

Myers, L. L., & Rittner, B. (1999). Family functioning and satisfaction of former residents of a non-therapeutic residential care facility. *Journal of Family Social Work, 3*(3), 53–68.

Myers, L. L., & Rittner, B. (2001). Adult psychosocial functioning of children raised in an orphanage. *Residential Treatment of Children and Youth, 18*(4), 3–21.

National Association of Social Workers. (1989). *NASW standards for the practice of clinical social work.* Silver Spring, MD: Author.

National Association of Social Workers. (1992). *NASW standards for school social work services.* Washington, DC: Author.

National Association of Social Workers. (1999). *Code of ethics.* Washington, DC: NASW Press.

Nezu, A. M., Ronan, G. F., Meadows, E. A., & McClure, K. (Eds.). (2000). *Practitioner's guide to empirically based measures of depression.* New York: Kluwer.

Normand, M. R., & Bailey, J. S. (2006). The effects of celeration lines on visual data analysis. *Behavior Modification, 30,* 295–314.

Northen, H. (1987). Assessment in direct practice. In A. Minahan (Ed.), *Encyclopedia of social work* (Vol. 1, pp. 171–183). Silver Spring, MD: NASW Press.

Pabian, W. E., Thyer, B. A., Straka, E., & Boyle, D. P. (2000). Do the families of children with developmental disabilities obtain recommended services? A follow-up study. *Journal of Human Behavior in the Social Environment, 3*(1), 45–58.

Perry, R. E. (2006). Do social workers make better child welfare workers than non-social workers? *Research on Social Work Practice, 15,* 1–14.

Pignotti, M. (2004). Thought field therapy in the media: A critical analysis of one exemplar. *Scientific Review of Mental Health Practice, 3*(2), 60–66.

Pignotti, M. (2005a). Callahan fails to meet the burden of proof for thought field therapy claims. [Comment]. *Journal of Clinical Psychology, 61,* 251–255.

Pignotti, M. (2005b). Thought field therapy voice technology vs. random meridian point sequences: A single-blind controlled experiment. *Scientific Review of Mental Health Practice, 4*(1), 38–47.

Pignotti, M. (2005c). Regarding the October 2002 Journal of Clinical Psychology special issue on thought field therapy: Retraction of conclusions of the article "Heart rate variability as an outcome measure for thought field therapy in clinical practice." [Comment]. *Journal of Clinical Psychology, 61,* 361–365.

Polster, R. A., & Collins, D. (1993). Structured observation. In R. M. Grinnell (Ed.), *Social work research and evaluation* (4th ed., pp. 244–261). Itasca, IL: F. E. Peacock.

Powers, E., & Witmer, H. (1951). *An experiment in the prevention of delinquency.* New York: Columbia University Press.

Preston, M. G., & Mudd, E. H. (1956). Research and service in social work: Conditions for a stable union. *Social Work, 1*(1), 34–40.

Reid, W. J. (2000). *The task planner: An intervention resource for human service professionals.* New York: Columbia University Press.

Richmond, M. (1917). *Social diagnosis.* New York: Russell Sage Foundation.

Roberts, A. R., & Greene, G. (Eds.). (2002). *Social workers' desk reference.* New York: Oxford University Press.

Robinson, R. M., Powers, J. M., Cleveland, P. H., & Thyer, B. A. (1990). Inpatient psychiatric treatment for depressed children and adolescents: Preliminary evaluations. *The Psychiatric Hospital, 21,* 107–112.

Rose, S. D. (1988). Practice experiments for doctoral dissertations: Research training and knowledge building. *Journal of Social Work Education, 24,* 115–122.

Rosen, A. (1983). Barriers to utilization of research by social work practitioners. *Journal of Social Service Research, 6*(3/4), 1–15.

Rosenberg, M. L., & Brody, R. (1974). The threat or challenge of accountability. *Social Work, 19,* 344–350.

Royse, D., Thyer, B. A., Padgett, D., & Logan, T. K. (2006). *Program evaluation: An introduction* (4th ed.). Belmont, CA: Thompson/Brooks-Cole.

Rubin, A., & Babbie, E. R. (1997). *Research methods for social work* (3rd ed.). Belmont, CA: Brooks/Cole.

Rubin, A., & Babbie, E. R. (2005). *Research methods for social work* (5th ed.). Belmont, CA: Brooks/Cole.

Rubin, A., & Conway, P. (1985). Standards for determining the magnitude of relationships in social work research. *Social Work Research and Abstracts, 21,* 34–39.

Schwartz, W., & Thyer, B. A. (2000). Partial hospitalization treatment for clinical depression: A pilot evaluation. *Journal of Human Behavior in the Social Environment, 3*(2), 13–21.

Scriven, M. (1999). The fine line between evaluation and explanation. *Research on Social Work Practice, 9,* 521–524.

Segal, S. (1972). Research on the outcome of social work intervention. *Journal of Health and Social Behavior, 13,* 3–17.

Shadish, W. R., Cook, T. D., & Campbell, D. T. (2002). *Experimental and quasi-experimental designs for generalized causal inference.* Boston: Houghton Mifflin.

Shyne, A. W. (1962). Casework research: Past and present. *Social Casework, 43,* 467–473.

Song, A. Y., & Gandhi, R. (1974). An analysis of behavior during the acquisition and maintenance phases of self-spoon-feeding skills of profound retardates. *Mental Retardation, 12,* 25–28.

Sowers-Hoag, K. M., Thyer, B. A., & Bailey, J. S. (1987). Promoting automobile safety belt use by young children. *Journal of Applied Behavior Analysis, 20,* 133–138.

Staats, A. W., & Butterfield, W. (1965). Treatment of non-reading in a culturally deprived juvenile delinquent: An application of reinforcement principles. *Child Development, 36,* 925–942.

Stocks, J. T. (1987). Estimating proportion of variance explained for selected analysis of variance designs. *Journal of Social Service Research, 11*(1), 77–91.

Stocks, J. T., & Williams, M. (1995). Evaluation of single-subject data using statistical hypothesis tests versus visual inspection of charts with and without celeration lines. *Journal of Social Service Research, 20,* 105–126.

Strupp, H., & Hadley, S. W. (1979). Specific versus nonspecific factors in psychotherapy: A controlled study of outcome. *Archives of General Psychiatry, 36,* 1125–1136.

Stuart, R. B. (1967). Behavioral control of overeating. *Behaviour Research and Therapy, 5,* 357–365.

Sutherland-Smith, G. P., Thyer, B. A., Clements, C., & Kropf, N. P. (1997). An evaluation of coalition building training for aging and developmental disability service providers. *Educational Gerontology, 23,* 105–111.

Thyer, B. A. (1981). Prolonged in-vivo exposure therapy with a 70-year-old woman. *Journal of Behavior Therapy and Experimental Psychiatry, 12,* 69–71.

Thyer, B. A. (1987). *Treating anxiety disorders.* Thousand Oaks, CA: Sage.

Thyer, B. A. (1988). Teaching without testing: A preliminary report of an innovative technique for social work education. *Innovative Higher Education, 13,* 47–53.

Thyer, B. A. (1991). Guidelines on evaluating outcome studies in social work practice. *Research on Social Work Practice, 1,* 76–91.

Thyer, B. A. (1992). Promoting evaluation research in the field of family preservation. In. E. S. Morton & R. K. Grigsby (Eds.), *Advancing family preservation practice* (pp. 13–149). Newbury Park, CA: Sage.

Thyer, B. A. (1994a). Are theories for practice necessary? *Journal of Social Work Education, 30,* 147–151.

Thyer, B. A. (1994b). *Successful publishing in scholarly journals.* Thousand Oaks, CA: Sage Publications.

Thyer, B. A. (1998). Promoting research on community practice: Using single system research designs. In R. H. MacNair (Ed.), *Research strategies for community practice* (pp. 47–61). Binghamton, NY: Haworth Press.

Thyer, B. A. (2001). What is the role of theory in research on social work practice? *Journal of Social Work Education, 37,* 9–25.

Thyer, B. A. (2002a). How to write up a social work outcome study for publication. *Journal of Social Work Research and Evaluation: An International Publication, 3,* 215–224.

Thyer, B. A. (2002b). Evaluation of social work practice in the new millennium: Myths and realities. In D. T. L. Shek, L. M. Chow, A. C. Fai, & J. J. Lee (Eds.), *Advances in social welfare in Hong Kong* (pp. 3–18). Hong Kong: The Chinese University Press.

Thyer, B. A. (2002c). Popper, positivism, and practice research. *Journal of Social Work Education, 38,* 471–474.

Thyer, B. A. (2005). A comprehensive listing of social work journals. *Research on Social Work Practice, 15,* 310–311.

Thyer, B. A. (2006). *Evidence-based macro-practice: Addressing the challenges and opportunities for social work education.* Paper presented at the Symposium on Improving the Teaching of Evidence-Based Practice, held at the University of Texas at Austin School of Social Work, Austin, TX, October 16–18.

Thyer, B. A., Artelt, T., & Shek, D. (2003). Using single-system research designs to evaluate practice: Potential applications for social work in Chinese contexts. *International Social Work, 46,* 163–176.

Thyer, B. A., & Birsinger, P. (1994). Treatment of clients with anxiety disorders. In D. K. Granvold (Ed.), *Cognitive and behavioral treatment: Methods and applications* (pp. 272–284). Belmont, CA: Brooks/Cole.

Thyer, B. A., & Curtis, G. C. (1983). The repeated pretest-posttest single-subject experiment: A new design for empirical clinical practice. *Journal of Behavior Therapy and Experimental Psychiatry, 14,* 311–315.

Thyer, B. A., Irvine, S., & Santa, C. A. (1984). Contingency management of exercise by chronic schizophrenics. *Perceptual and Motor Skills, 58,* 419–425.

Thyer, B. A., & Myers, L. L. (2007). Research in evidence-based social work. In T. Ronen & A. Freeman (Eds.), *Cognitive behavior therapy in clinical social work* (pp. 45–66). New York: Springer.

Thyer, B. A., Papsdorf, J. D., Davis, R. L., & Vallecorsa, S. (1984). Autonomic correlates of the Subjective Anxiety Scale. *Journal of Behavior Therapy and Experimental Psychiatry, 15,* 3–7.

Thyer, B. A., Papsdorf, J. D., Himle, D., McCann, M., Caldwell, S., & Wickert, M. (1981). In-vivo distraction coping training in the treatment of test anxiety. *Journal of Clinical Psychology, 37,* 754–764.

Thyer, B. A., Papsdorf, J. D., & Wright, P. (1984). Physiological and psychological effects of acute intentional hyperventilation. *Behaviour Research and Therapy, 22,* 587–590.

Thyer, B. A., Sowers-Hoag, K. M., & Love, J. P. (1986). The influence of field instructor-student gender combinations on student perceptions of field instruction quality. *Arete, 11*(2), 25–30.

Thyer, B. A., Sutphen, R., & Sowers-Hoag, K. M. (1990). Using structured study questions as a teaching method in social work education: Initial validation studies. *Innovative Higher Education, 14,* 155–164.

Thyer, B. A., & Thyer, K. B. (1992). Single-system research designs in social work practice: A bibliography from 1965 to 1990. *Research on Social Work Practice, 2,* 99–116.

Thyer, B. A., Thyer, K., & Massa, S. (1991). Behavioral analysis and therapy in gerontology. In P. K. H. Kim (Ed.), *Serving the elderly: Skills for practice* (pp. 117–135). New York: Aldine DeGruyter.

Thyer, B. A., & Vonk, M. E. (2007). Evidence-based practice: Behaviorism. In B. Thomlison & K. Corcoran (Eds.), *Evidence-based internship: A skills-based manual.* New York: Oxford University Press.

Thyer, B. A., Vonk, M. E., & Tandy, C. C. (1996). Are advanced standing and two-year program MSW students equivalently prepared? A comparison of BSW licensure examination scores. *Arete, 20*(4), 42–46.

Thyer, B. A., & Westhuis, D. (1989). Test-retest reliability of the Clinical Anxiety Scale. *Phobia Practice and Research Journal, 2,* 113–115.

Tripodi, T. (1994). *A primer on single-subject design for clinical social workers.* Washington, DC: NASW Press.

Valentine, P. V., & Smith, T. E. (2001). Evaluating traumatic incident reduction therapy with female inmates: A randomized controlled clinical trial. *Research on Social Work Practice, 11,* 40–52.

van Senden Theis, S. (1924). *How foster children turn out.* New York: State Charities Aid Association.

Vonk, M. E., & Thyer, B. A. (1995). Exposure therapy in the treatment of vaginal penetration phobia: A single-case evaluation. *Journal of Behavior Therapy and Experimental Psychiatry, 26,* 359–363.

Vonk, M. E., & Thyer, B. A. (1999). Evaluating the effectiveness of short-term treatment at a university counseling center. *Journal of Clinical Psychology, 55,* 1095–1106.

Vonk, M. E., Zucrow, E., & Thyer, B. A. (1996). Female MSW students' satisfaction with practicum supervision: The effect of supervisor gender. *Journal of Social Work Education, 32,* 415–419.

Waite, W. L., & Holder, M. D. (2003). Assessment of the emotional freedom technique: An alternative treatment of fear. *Scientific Review of Mental Health Practice, 2*(1), 20.

Weinbach, R. W. (1989). When is statistical significance meaningful? A practice perspective. *Journal of Sociology and Social Welfare, 16*(1), 31–37.

Weiss, B., Catron, T., Harris, V., & Phung, T. M. (1999). The effectiveness of traditional child psychotherapy. *Journal of Consulting and Clinical Psychology, 67,* 82–94.

Westhuis, D., & Thyer, B. A. (1989). Development and validation of the Clinical Anxiety Scale. *Educational and Psychological Measurement, 49,* 153–163.

Williams, M., Thyer, B. A., Bailey, J. S., & Harrison, D. F. (1989). Promoting safety belt use with traffic signs and prompters. *Journal of Applied Behavior Analysis, 22,* 71–76.

Wilson, P. G., Reid, D. H., Phillips, J. F., & Burgio, L. D. (1984). Normalization of institutional mealtimes for profoundly retarded persons: Effects and noneffects of teaching family-style dining. *Journal of Applied Behavior Analysis, 17,* 189–201.

Wolpe, J. (1958). *Psychotherapy by reciprocal inhibition.* Stanford, CA: Stanford University Press.

About the Authors

Bruce A. Thyer received his MSW from the University of Georgia and his PhD in social work and psychology from the University of Michigan. He is currently a professor of social work at Florida State University in Tallahassee.

Laura L. Myers received her MSW and PhD in social work from the University of Georgia. She is an assistant professor of social work at Thomas University in Thomasville, Georgia. Thyer is editor and Myers is managing editor of the bimonthly journal *Research on Social Work Practice.*

Index